SECRET TO THE SCIENCE OF GETTING RICH

Secret to the Science of Getting Rich

SHIRLEY SMOLKO, MBA, MSA
Fenwicke Holmes, Wallace Wattles

Cavallaro Publishing

CONTENTS

Part 2: Fenwicke Holmes

Part 3: Wallace Wattles

Preface

Conclusion

Printed in the U.S.A.

First Printing, 2022

Second Printing, 2023

ISBN: 978-1-958104-01-9

Library of Congress Control Number: 2022907834

Cavallaro Publishing
North Venice, Florida
www.cavallaropub.com
cavallaropub@gmail.com

DISCLAIMER

This book contains material from a distant time that may not be gender neutral or sensitive. Therefore, all pronouns shall be deemed to refer to the masculine, feminine, neuter, singular, or plural; wherever used herein, a pronoun in the masculine gender shall be considered to include the feminine gender.

The publisher and the author do not make any guarantee or other promise as to any results that may be obtained from using the content of this book. To the maximum extent permitted by law, the publisher and the author disclaim any and all liability in the event any information, commentary, analysis, opinions, advice, or recommendations contained in this book prove to be inaccurate, incomplete, or unreliable or result in any losses.

In summary, you understand that we make absolutely no guarantees regarding income as a result of applying this information, as well as the fact that you are solely responsible for the results of any action taken on your part as a result of any given information.

Introduction By
Shirley Smolko

In New Thought literature, poverty is often referred to as a mental disease. If you are suffering from it, then you are a victim of it. In 2021, there were over 43 million poor people in the United States. Most of these individuals don't see a way out of poverty, so they become content with their lot in life. They may work hard, but they have lost hope of ever being financially independent. Many people keep themselves poor because they believe they will never have enough to live on. The thoughts we have are projections of our beliefs. Because thoughts manifest reality, poverty thoughts become objectified, thereby perpetuating the experience and belief in lack.

The minds of children in most impoverished families are saturated with poverty thoughts. They see poverty-stricken conditions everywhere. They hear everybody talking about limitation, lack, and oppression. Everything in their experience suggests poverty. Is it any wonder that children brought up in such an atmosphere repeat the poverty-stricken conditions of their parents and environment?

Prosperity begins in the mind, therefore, no one can become prosperous while they expect to remain poor. Also, we get what we expect, so if we expect nothing, we'll get nothing. To be prosperous, we must maintain an attitude of faith and optimism. Faith is a confident expectation of that which you intentionally set out to demonstrate. If your goal is to make a million dollars in your first year of business, then you must have faith that you will reach your goal. Optimism is essential; it is to the individual what the sun is to vegetation. It is the sunshine of the mind, which constructs life, beauty, and growth within everything in its reach. Our mental faculties grow and thrive in it just as plants and trees grow and thrive in the sunshine.

The greatest power in the world is the power of our thoughts. Nothing exists that did not first exist in thought, from the first sun that blazed only in the Mind of the Creator to the first airplane created in the minds of the Wright brothers.

Mind in action is called the law of cause and effect. Law is the principle on which the mind works. Thought is the first cause, and form is the effect. Thoughts act upon substance to produce things. Substance is pure energy with the potential to become whatever we impress upon it. The things created by our thoughts maintain form and reality for as long as they are sustained by the original thought. Therefore, the secret to *The Science of Getting Rich* is knowing how to form and sustain energy with thoughts that create wealth, along with acting in a certain way by connecting thought with personal action. For instance, you must open a channel for riches to flow to you—such as a business or investment—if you expect to get rich!

Part 1: Shirley Smolko

The First Cause of Money

The Substance of Mind

Portal to the Supreme Power of the Universe

You Reap the Money Thoughts you Sow

~ 1 ~

THE FIRST CAUSE OF MONEY

The First Cause of money can be used by anyone—orthodox or liberal, religious or nonreligious. In the words of the great inventor and scientist, Thomas A. Edison, "All scientists, in getting nearer and nearer the first great cause, feel that about and through everything there is the play of an eternal mind."

It is this First Cause—the Original Force—that moves the planets, starts life on earth, animates the body, builds houses, puts souls into men, and makes people think. The soul of man—the part of us that survives physical death—is an emanation of the Original Force of the Universe. If it were possible to stop this vitalizing force in the Universe, everything, including man, would chill, wither, and die.

So then, it is the presence of the Original Force throughout the world that warms, invigorates, enlivens, and makes vital what would otherwise be cold, dead, and empty. It is this potent force that warms the soil in the springtime, sends sap up the trees, causes buds to bloom, perfumes flowers, and colors their beautiful petals. Everything that exists in life is an expression of the Original Force.

In his book, Creative Mind & Success, Earnest Homes wrote the following passage about the expression of life and how it relates to money:

If all is an expression of life, then *money* is an expression of life and, as such, must be good. Without a certain amount of it in our lives, we would have a hard time. But how to get it—that is the human race's problem. How will we acquire wealth? Money didn't make itself, and not being self-creative, it must have an effect. Behind it must be the Cause that projects it. That cause is never seen; no cause is ever seen. Consciousness is a cause, and people who have a money consciousness have the outward expression of it. People who have it as a sure reality in their minds also have it as an expression in their pockets. People who don't have this mental likeness don't have money in their pockets.

What we need to do is acquire a money consciousness. This may seem very material, but the true idea of money is not material—it is spiritual. We need to make our unity with it. We can never do this while we hold it away from us by thinking that we don't have it. Let us change the method and begin to make our unity with supply by daily declaring that all the Power in the Universe is daily bringing to us all that we can use. Feel the presence of supply. Know that it is yours now.

The study of quantum physics suggests that the nature of primal substance (or ether) is that all its particles are in perfect equilibrium or balance. The only way this balance can be disturbed and brought into form is by the application of some immaterial force to primal substance. In his paper, *Man's Greatest Achievement*, Nikola Tesla wrote:

The primary substance, thrown into infinitesimal whirls of prodigious velocity, becomes gross matter; the force subsides, the motion ceases, and matter disappears, reverting to the primary substance.

We must therefore posit that a power brought about by will, or an act of Mind, is the only possible immaterial force. In his book *Thought Power, Sri* Swami Sivananda wrote:

> Thought is the greatest force on earth. Thought is the most powerful weapon in the armor of a Yogi. Constructive thought transforms, renews and builds. The far-reaching possibilities of this force were most accurately developed to perfection by the ancients and put to the highest possible use.

> For, thought is the primal force at the origin and back of all creation; the genesis of the entire phenomenal creation is given as a single thought that arose in the Cosmic Mind.

> The world is the Primal Idea made manifest. This First Thought became manifest as a vibration issuing from the Eternal Stillness of the Divine Essence. This is the reference in classic terminology to the Ichha, desire of the Hiranyagarbha, Cosmic Soul, that originates as a Spandana or vibration.

> This vibration is nothing like the rapid oscillation to and fro of physical particles, but is something infinitely subtle, so subtle as to be even inconceivable to the normal mind. But this has made it clear that all forces are ultimately resolvable into a state of pure vibration. Modern science also has newly arrived at this conclusion after its prolonged researches in external physical nature.

Later in the book, he goes on to say:

> Thought is a vital, living dynamic power–the most vital, subtle and irresistible force existing in the universe. Through the instrumentality of thought you acquire creative power. Thought passes from one man to another. It influences

people; a man of powerful thought can influence readily people of weak thoughts.

Life can only come from Life, and motion can only have its origin in the mind. The word spirit comes from the Latin root 'spiro' which is also the Italian word for 'I breathe. Therefore, the universe springs from the outbreathing of the Mind. This is the expansive movement of spirit with which ancient philosophers deal so much. We are told in the book of Genesis, chapter one, verse two, that "The spirit of God moved on the face of the waters." The word "waters" is the esoteric term for Mind or Creative Mind. The Word acts on the mind to produce substance in the visible universe and then to bring that substance into varied forms, in sun, moon, stars, land, sea, vegetation, and man.

~ 2 ~

THE SUBSTANCE OF MIND

P sychologist discovered long ago that the mind of man can be divided into two basic parts, the conscious and subconscious, as shown in the following diagram:

The Total Mind
Shirley Smolko

THE CONSCIOUS MIND

T he conscious part of your mind—which comprises only ten percent of your total mind—is the part that tastes, hears, smells, feels, sees, talks, thinks, decides, laughs, cries, and plays. It is the waking mind—in contrast to the subconscious mind—which, compared with the conscious mind, seems asleep. In other words, the conscious mind is the "active" part of the total mind, and it can direct and control the subconscious mind, which is "passive" and ready to receive direction from the conscious.

The conscious part of man's mind is the storehouse of his external knowledge, the seat of that intelligence through which he exercises his sense of reasoning, analyzing, and willing. The conscious intelligence is directly and indirectly influenced by some or all of the five physical senses. As long as these senses are active, the conscious mind cannot be restrained from reasoning since reasoning is its normal function.

THE SUBCONSCIOUS MIND

The subconscious mind automatically directs the functions of the body that go on without the direction or knowledge of the conscious mind. The Latin prefix "sub" means underneath; hence, "subconscious" mind means the mind underneath the conscious mind. Your subconscious mind is responsible for the respiration of your lungs, the contraction of your heart, the rebuilding of the millions of tiny cells that make up your body, and the function of all your internal organs. It also directs your dreams, as well as other important aspects of your mentality. It is the seat of deeper constructive thought, memory, feelings, courage or fear, and instincts. It is also the nucleus of habitual happiness or chronic sorrow, hope or despair, good or bad motives, and the hidden resources for health, happiness, and success. The center of the higher spiritual faculties of the soul, such as intuition and moral sense, lies within the subconscious mind. It is the throne of God within us—the powerhouse of the Universe—which is continuously manifesting our deepest beliefs. Instead of manifesting continuously by default, we can consciously tap this power to manifest our desires intentionally by reprogramming the subconscious mind with new beliefs.

When an impulse originates in the subconscious mind and rises to seek expression in the conscious mind, it crosses what has been called the "threshold of consciousness"—that imaginary line that separates consciousness from subconsciousness. You can just as easily direct ideas DOWN from your conscious mind into your subconscious mind as you can receive ideas UP from your subconscious mind.

THE CONSCIOUS MIND CAN CHOOSE

Whatever is observed through the senses of sight, smell, touch, taste, or hearing immediately conveys a definite impression to the conscious mind, which, having the power of will (and therefore the privilege of selection), can either accept or reject the impression. If the impression is accepted, it is instantly passed down to the subconscious mind for adoption. The subconscious mind then embraces the impression—whether good or evil—because the subconscious mind is not capable of analytical reasoning. It is controlled by the conscious mind. Therefore, you can readily see how important it is to maintain positive thoughts if you wish to exert a beneficial influence on your subconscious mind.

So the field of operations of the conscious mind is chiefly confined to what it perceives through the senses, and it is through the senses that it insists upon receiving proof. The conscious mind takes nothing for granted. But, once thoroughly satisfied, it conveys whatever may be its final convictions and conclusions to the subconscious mind, which, being unable to reason inductively, accepts them without the slightest resistance, whether they be correct and helpful or faulty and destructive.

Therefore, be very careful that you allow nothing harmful, depressing, discouraging, or unhealthy to reach your subconscious mind. Remember—it is impossible to convey any impression whatsoever to your subconscious mind without the impression first being accepted by your conscious mind. This is so, as already explained, because the conscious mind stands like a sentinel on guard at the entrance to your inner faculties and forbids the passing in of any idea unacceptable to it.

THE SUBCONSCIOUS IS AN OBEDIENT SERVANT

The subconscious mind freely accepts all suggestions furnished to it by the conscious mind, as clearly expounded by Mr. A. L. Allen in his *Message of New Thought:*

> *Through the law of suggestion, the subconscious, or subjective, mind submits to the thoughts and impressions it receives from the conscious, or objective, mind. These suggestions may be given either by yourself or by someone else. The subconscious mind registers the impression, which, over time, is given expression in the life and character of the individual. The subconscious mind will faithfully reproduce every mental idea or state contained in the impression. It is a rich soil, and the seed-thought planted in it by the conscious mind will produce according to its kind. If we plant flowers, we'll get flowers. If we sow tares, the crop will be tares. The subconscious is an obedient servant. It obeys the thoughts of the conscious mind. What it receives, it reproduces, and its effect is manifested in the personality of the individual. If we sow ideas of disease, we shall reap a harvest of disease. Thoughts of health will be re-expressed in healthy conditions. If we sow ideas of poverty, that will be our portion. If we sow thoughts of inferiority, weakness, and fear, we shall build a personality devoid of character and strength. Ideals of abundance will produce abundance if we enforce them with intelligence and energy.*

In his *Handbook of New Thought*, Mr. Horatio W. Dresser, states it this way:

> The conscious mind observes facts, and applies them to general principles. The subconscious mind does not reason, but it receives and registers all impressions and affirmations suggested to it.

The perceptions of reality received throughout one's life, through some or all of the physical senses, are the chief means for influencing the convictions of the subconscious mind. Each subsequent experience changes one's point of view to some degree. The things we see, the words we hear, the books we read, etc., are all parts of the material world that help determine the standpoint from which the subconscious mind reacts. Therefore, if the subconscious mind is trained through helpful ideas, good consequences will follow, but if it is permitted to absorb unhealthy ideas, injury will result in direct proportion to the individual's natural susceptibility. A phrase often used in computer jargon, "Garbage In; Garbage Out," is a wonderful analogy of how we program our subconscious minds with unhealthy ideas and beliefs, often without even realizing it. If we program our minds with ideas and beliefs of lack and limitation, we will express poverty. On the other hand, if we program our minds with ideas and beliefs of abundance and opportunity, we will express wealth.

~ 3 ~

PORTAL TO THE SUPREME
POWER OF THE UNIVERSE

Prentice Mulford wrote about the Supreme Power of the Universe in several of his books, however, the following except was taken from his book, *The Gift of The Spirit*:

A Supreme Power and Wisdom govern the Universe. The Supreme Mind is measureless and pervades endless space. The Supreme Wisdom, Power, and Intelligence are in everything that exists from the atom to the planet.

The Supreme Power and Wisdom are more than in everything. The Supreme Mind is everything. The Supreme Mind is every atom of the mountain, the sea, the tree, the bird, the animal, the man, the woman. The Supreme Wisdom cannot be understood by man or by beings superior to man. But man will gladly receive the Supreme Thought and its wisdom, and let it work for happiness through him, caring not to fathom its mystery.

The Supreme Power has us in its charge, as it has the suns and endless systems of worlds in space. As we grow more to recognize this sublime and exhaustless wisdom, we shall learn more and more to demand that wisdom, draw it to ourselves, make it a part of ourselves, and thereby be ever making ourselves newer and newer. This means ever perfecting health, greater and greater power to enjoy all that exists, gradual transition into a higher state of being and the development of powers which we do not now realize as belonging to us.

Ralph Waldo Emerson wrote the following about our access to this power in the seventh chapter of his book *Nature:*

> Who can set bounds to the possibilities of man? Once inhale the upper air, being admitted to behold the absolute natures of justice and truth, and we learn that man has access to the entire mind of the Creator, is himself the creator in the finite. This view, which admonishes me where the sources of wisdom and power lie, and points to virtue as to the golden key, which opens the palace of eternity,

There is one temple in the universe, and that is the body of man. We are the miracle of miracles, the great, indescribable mystery of God. This miracle is wrapped up in the mystery of life, of which the conscious and subconscious workings of the mind are two of its most marvelous expressions. It is through the subconscious that we put ourselves in communion with the Universal Mind. It has been said that the Subconscious Mind is the great ocean of mental life, while the Conscious Mind is merely the ripple that washes against the shore. The fact that the subconscious mind is in communion with the great Universal Mind should fill us with a sense of confidence, power, and unlimited possibilities.

How can we tap into this unlimited World Force of the Universal Mind? As we have already seen, the subconscious mind is open to suggestions made by the conscious mind. Being immeasurably sensitive to impressions from without, the subconscious is incessantly receptive and subject to the influence of the conscious mind when the latter is awake. In a figurative sense, the subconscious mind is the moving picture film or daily journal of the mind. It knows things, but it does not know how it knows them. It is the believing and faith mind, for it believes without requiring evidence. Being the embodiment of truth, it neither doubts nor asks questions but takes everything stated for granted. It is the truthful, hopeful, trusting mind—the mind that predominates in the simple life of the child, for instance.

~ 4 ~

YOU REAP THE MONEY
THOUGHTS YOU SOW

M any people are sincere in their desire to attain success in life but unwilling to contribute the mental elements necessary to realize it. Furthermore, they often prevent its realization through counterproductive beliefs and negative thoughts. All things are governed by an established energetic (spiritual) law. According to that law, every tree bears fruit after its kind, and every seed sown produces no other than its own kind. Likewise, if the condition of your conscious mind is positive and harmonious, it cannot help but produce good and beneficial results. On the contrary, if the seeds of fear, doubt, and inferiority are sown, don't expect to reap a MONEY HARVEST! In you exist all possibilities, so make the decision from this moment on that you will tap the unlimited riches of your subconscious mind.

BANISH FEARFUL THOUGHTS OF LACK & LIMITATION

F ear, that instinctive source of most evil—together with the lower emotions—is often stimulated by a conscious mind that has been nurtured by false ideas and beliefs. Fear distorts the mind's reasoning, rendering it imperfect. When faced with obstacles and difficulties in life, do not look upon such hindrances as unusual; rather, consider their presence perfectly natural under the circumstances and determine to overcome them. Do not allow the conscious mind to become uneasy and magnify them through an alarmed reasoning process. If you do, you are, through your own needless fear, helping to create failure.

Train your conscious mind to shield you from harmful influences. Its chief office is to reason intelligently and thus protect your subconscious mind by rejecting every injurious suggestion. It should also be trained to admit all helpful suggestions and permit your subconscious mind to receive them.

TURN AWAY FROM ADVERSE SUGGESTIONS

Not only is the subconscious mind susceptible to the influence of the conscious mind, but it is also susceptible to suggestions conveyed to it by others. Therefore, don't expose yourself to the negativity of others. Your conscious mind, which stands on guard at the entrance to your subconscious, must decide which suggestions may enter your subconscious. Only suggestions that are constructive and helpful—no matter how improbable they may seem—should be allowed to enter your subconscious mind.

Don't reason yourself out of the things to which you are entitled mentally, physically, and materially. "Can't" shouldn't be in your vocabulary. Affirm with all the positive force in you that an abundance of money to enjoy life is your birthright.

THINK POSITIVE MONEY THOUGHTS

Your thought is strong and potent beyond measure, but when you assume the 'wanting' attitude, although you do most certainly attract, it is nothing like the powerful attraction formed by your quiet, confident attitude of absolute conviction that the thing wants you. The attitude of desire is strong, but the attitude of certainty and possession—which this new thought makes possible—is a wonderful and veritable tower of strength. It has made possible for me things that had previously been impossible.

It is impossible to realize success with money if you continually expect failure. Do not entertain thoughts that are destructive or contrary to your desires. The thoughts you think are constantly being registered in your highly receptive subconscious mind—to haunt you later. Anxiety and doubt about your ability to attract money show that you have not accepted the fact that money wants you. Money cannot come to you until you have accepted this concept as a reality, so let go of any anxiety or apprehension that you may have regarding money. Rest in confidence, knowing that your subconscious mind is your own *genie in a bottle* and is able to manifest anything you desire.

Part 2: Fenwicke Holmes

Matter or Thought in Form

Ether and Cosmic Mind

Thought and Form

~ 5 ~

MATTER OR THOUGHT IN FORM

W hat we seek to do in this chapter is show that the substance we call "matter" is simply a grouping of particles of energy, or electrons," and that these electrons or energy are created by thought. This can be shown by experiments that have been made with the mind of the individual, which reveal the fact that his thoughts either create energy or put it into purposeful activity. Then we want to show that the form things take is in response to a corresponding thought. When we understand that the material of which things are made is thought-energy or vibration and that it can be molded into form by the thoughts we think, we are prepared to realize that the world we live in is very real and that what we need to do is not deny it but to understand it in order to be masters of our bodies and conditions.

Physical science traces matter back to its origin in a primary substance, which it calls ether. This ether pervades all space everywhere, and there is no place where it cannot be found. Ether is simply a name given to that which can neither be seen, felt, tasted, nor actually examined scientifically, yet the necessity of the case posits its omnipresence. It is a frictionless, pulseless, motionless medium until it is moved by some form of energy.

Thought and Energy or Matter

When a visible universe comes into existence, it begins with a movement of some sort within the invisible ether. Science speaks of the movement as the activity of "vortex rings" or whirling particles of energy which gradually coalesce into nebulae or vapors; and these violently throw out vast fragments into the ether to congeal into planets and systems. Such activity can be seen even at this day in the nebulae of Andromeda where a new universe is in process of creation.

Science therefore perceives that the visible universe is composed of infinitely small particles of energy called electrons. These electrons are the same kind whether in a planet, the wood in a table, or the brains in a man's head, a fact which may seem highly uncomplimentary to the latter (technically the electron is not a "particle" but a property of matter). The difference between "substances" is then merely the difference in the number of particles to a given area and the rate of their motion.

These infinitely fine energized particles coalesce sufficiently to form the various things which we call mineral, animal, or vegetable substance. But they never actually coalesce into an indivisible unit for we discover that each atom of energy is separate from every other and that indeed each is as widely separated from the other according to its size as the planets. are according to their size and that there is a further similarity from the fact that each atom revolves upon its own axis. The "world of matter" therefore is really a world of energy and so-called substance is vibration.

Since we live in a world of energy, since the substance of the universe is really energy, the problem of science and philosophy alike has been to account for the first presence of energy in ether. What force moved upon or within ether to give the vortex rings their first impulse? Many physical scientists now declare that the explanation is metaphysical or due to the act of a Will or Mind. The student may therefore wisely engage his attention in solving this problem.

~ 6 ~

ETHER AND COSMIC MIND

The difficulty of explaining the origin of the universe is easily dissolved by the mental scientist, who perceives the so-called ether as merely another name for the Cosmic Mind. The physical scientist's description of ether exactly corresponds with the mental scientist's explanation of Mind or Universal Creative Intelligence. The movement that results in electrons and vortex rings is the movement of the Divine Will within the Cosmic Mind; in other words, the Mind thinks, and thinking creates energy, and energy in the form of electrons produces a universe.

When the creation of a cosmos begins, a convulsive movement takes place in selected areas, and the primary energy of a universe appears. The universe in which we live, therefore, is to be conceived of as thought and the whole existing cosmos as Mind in Action. The universe is created by some power resident within. It is made out of the Mind; or, in other words, Spirit makes things by becoming the things it makes. Substance, in its last analysis, is intelligence. Therefore, thought turns into things. "The Word is made flesh and dwells among us." Since substance is intelligence, it is governed by intelligence. Since the foundation of the world is the Mind, it must be one.

This should clarify the thoughts of the student as to the part he may play in the Divine Plan, for if Spirit produces a world by becoming that world, then we produce the thing we desire by becoming that thing. Practically speaking, it means nothing less than our ability to rule our world and, by our thinking, cause the things we desire to assemble themselves around us. Carrying this to the ultimate of the power inherent in us, it means that as Jesus materialized from the atmosphere the bread and fish, so may the enlightened consciousness some day aspire to rule his world. If we cannot today use the full power of the Sons of God, we can at least expect that our bodies will yield to our will, our environment will reflect our mental attitudes, and material possessions will come into our hands. And to as many as receive, He gives them the power to become the sons of God. This is the truth, which, if known, will make us free.

~ 7 ~

THOUGHT AND FORM

It now remains for us to show that thought gives form to substance, a fact that is demonstrated without difficulty once the foregoing principle is known. As we have learned, creation is the growth, unfoldment, or expansion of the "principle of life" from within. That which we call life or intelligence, then, first produces energy or vibration, of which the visible universe or cosmos is composed. On the other hand, the visible universe everywhere manifests itself in form. Since Mind is the primary power, since it creates particles of energy, and since these particles of energy everywhere group themselves in form, only one conclusion is possible: Thought Molds Substance into Form.

It is a principle inherent in Nature itself that Substance should assume harmonious forms. This is illustrated in the snowflakes, which fall in varied, flower-like patterns from the silent sky. Or one may study the tendency in an interesting experiment in musical vibration. Grains of sand sprinkled on a piece of plate glass, properly poised, will draw together into beautiful geometric figures when the bow of a violin is drawn across the edge of the glass, and each musical vibration will change the form the sand assumes.

As wonderful as these experiments are, they are scarcely comparable with the thousand unnoticed miracles of creation around us. Examine the formative power of creative thought in an acorn.

In that frail shell, a mighty oak lies cradled, and an instinctive intelligence will unfold its life into definite form.

Turn to the stars and study the inner tendency of all matter to coalesce, to rotate, and to assume spherical form, and then turn back to the other end of the creative scale and examine the development of human life. Within the fetus is the sleepless and mysterious intelligence, which we call the subconscious mind, which produces the matchless and intricate mechanisms that someday will be in the form of man.

Do we not perceive, therefore, that the substance of the invisible universe is mind, that thought produces energy or the substance of the visible universe by acting upon the invisible, and again, that thought molds this energy or matter into form? We are led, therefore, to the inevitable conclusion that the Existing Cosmos Is Thought in Form; that it exists and moves in the limitless sea of the non-manifested Mind; and that potential power lies in that Mind to create new universes and new forms when and where It will.

Part 3: Wallace Wattles

The Right to be Rich

There is a Science to Getting Rich

Is Opportunity Monopolized?

The First Principle in the Science of Getting Rich

Increasing Life

How Riches Come to You

Gratitude

Thinking in a Certain Way

Preface

This book is pragmatical, not philosophical; a practical manual, not a treatise upon theories. It is intended for the men and women whose most pressing need is for money; who wish to get rich first, and philosophize afterward. It is for those who have, so far, found neither the time, the means, nor the opportunity to go deeply into the study of metaphysics, but who want results and who are willing to take the conclusions of science as a basis for action, without going into all the processes by which those conclusions were reached.

It is expected that the reader will take the fundamental statements upon faith, just as he would take statements concerning a law of electrical action if they were promulgated by a Marconi or an Edison; and, taking the statements upon faith, that he will prove their truth by acting upon them without fear or hesitation. Every man or woman who does this will certainly get rich; for the science herein applied is an exact science, and failure is impossible. For the benefit, however, of those who wish to investigate philosophical theories and so secure a logical basis for faith, I will here cite certain authorities.

The monistic theory of the universe—the theory that One is All, and that All is One; that one Substance manifests itself as the seeming many elements of the material world—is of Hindu origin, and has been gradually winning its way into the thought of the western world for two hundred years. It is the foundation of all the Oriental philosophies, and of those of Descartes, Spinoza, Leibnitz, Schopenhauer, Hegel, and Emerson.

The reader who would dig to the philosophical foundations is advised to read Hegel and Emerson; and he will do well to read "The Eternal News," a very excellent pamphlet published by J. J. Brown, 300 Cathcart Road, Govanhill, Glasgow, Scotland. He may also find some help in a series of articles written by the author, which were published in Nautilus (Holyoke, Mass.) during the spring and summer of 1909, under the title "What is Truth?"

In writing this book I have sacrificed all other considerations to plainness and simplicity of style, so that all might understand. The plan of action laid down herein was deduced from the conclusions of philosophy; it has been thoroughly tested, and bears the supreme test of practical experiment; it works. If you wish to know how the conclusions were arrived at, read the writings of the authors mentioned above; and if you wish to reap the fruits of their philosophies in actual practice, read this book and do exactly as it tells you to do.

The Author.

~ 8 ~

THE RIGHT TO BE RICH

Whatever may be said in praise of poverty, the fact remains that it is not possible to live a really complete or successful life unless one is rich. You cannot rise to your greatest possible height in talent or soul development unless you have plenty of money. To unfold the soul and develop talent, you must have many things to use, and you cannot have these things unless you have money to buy them with.

Man develops in mind, soul, and body by making use of things, and society is so organized that we must have money in order to become the possessor of things; therefore, the basis of all advancement for us must be the science of getting rich.

The object of all life is development, and everything that lives has an inalienable right to all the development it is capable of attaining.

Man's right to life means his right to have the free and unrestricted use of all the things which may be necessary to his fullest mental, spiritual, and physical unfoldment; or, in other words, his right to be rich fullest mental, spiritual, and physical unfoldment; or, in other words, his right to be rich.

In this book, I will not speak of riches in a figurative way; to be really rich does not mean to be satisfied or content with a little. No one ought to be satisfied with a little if they are capable of using and enjoying more. The purpose of Nature is the advancement and un-foldment of life, and everyone should have all that can contribute to the power, elegance, beauty, and richness of life; to be content with less is sinful.

People who own all they want in order to live a full life are rich, and those who do not have plenty of money might not be able to ex-perience the things they want. Life has advanced so far and become so complex that even the most ordinary man or woman requires a great amount of wealth in order to live in a manner that even approaches completeness. Every person naturally wants to become all that they are capable of becoming. This desire to realize innate possibilities is inherent in human nature—we cannot help wanting to be all that we can be.

Success in life is becoming what you want to be. You can become what you want to be only by making use of things, and you can have the free use of things only as you become rich enough to buy them. To understand *The Science of Getting Rich* is, therefore, the most essential of all knowledge.

There is nothing wrong in wanting to get rich. The desire for riches is really the desire for a richer, fuller, and more abundant life—and that desire is praiseworthy. The person who does not desire to live more abundantly is abnormal, and so the individual who does not desire to have money enough to buy all he wants is abnormal.

There are three motives for which we live:

1. We live for the body.
2. We live for the mind.
3. We live for the soul.

No one of these is better or holier than the other; all are equally desirable, and no one of the three—body, mind, or soul—can live fully if either of the others is cut short of full life and expression. It is not right or noble to live only for the soul and deny mind or body, and it is wrong to live for the intellect and deny body and soul.

We are all acquainted with the loathsome consequences of living for the body and denying both mind and soul, and we see that real life means the complete expression of all that we can give forth through body, mind, and soul. You cannot be really happy or satisfied unless your body is living fully in every function, and unless the same is true of your mind and soul. Wherever there is unexpressed possibility or function not performed, there is unsatisfied desire. Desire is possibility seeking expression or function seeking performance.

We cannot live fully in body without good food, comfortable clothing, and warm shelter, and without freedom from excessive toil. Rest and recreation are also necessary to this physical life.

We cannot live fully in mind without books and time to study them, without opportunity for travel and observation, or without intellectual companionship.

To live fully in mind, we must have intellectual recreations and must surround ourselves with all the objects of art and beauty we are capable of using and appreciating.

To live fully in the soul, we must have love, and love is denied expression by poverty.

Our highest happiness is found in the bestowal of benefits on those we love, and love finds its most natural and spontaneous expression in giving. The individual who has nothing to give cannot fill their place as a husband, wife, father, mother, or as a citizen. It is, therefore, of supreme importance for us to be rich.

It is perfectly right that you should desire to be rich; if you are a normal man or woman, you cannot help doing so. It is perfectly right that you should give your best attention to the Science of Getting Rich, for it is the noblest and most necessary of all studies. If you neglect this study, you are derelict in your duty to yourself, to God, and to humanity; for you can render God and humanity no greater service than to make the most of yourself.

~ 9 ~

THERE IS A SCIENCE TO
GETTING RICH

There is a Science of getting rich, and it is an exact science, like algebra or arithmetic. There are certain laws which govern the process of acquiring riches. When these laws are learned and obeyed, you will get rich with mathematical certainty.

The ownership of money and property comes as a result of doing things in a certain way; those who do things in this Certain Way—whether on purpose or accidentally—get rich, while those who do not do things in this Certain Way—no matter how hard they work or how able they are—remain poor.

It is a natural law that like causes always produce like effects. Therefore, any man or woman who learns to do things in this Certain Way will infallibly get rich.

That the above statement is true is shown by the following facts:

Fact #1

Getting rich is not a matter of environment, for if it were, all the people in certain neighborhoods would become wealthy; the people of one city would all be rich, while those of other towns would all be poor; or the inhabitants of one state would roll in wealth, while those of an adjoining state would be in poverty.

But everywhere we see rich and poor living side by side, in the same environment, and often engaged in the same vocations. When two people are in the same locality and in the same business and one gets rich while the other remains poor, it shows that getting rich is not primarily a matter of environment. Some environments may be more favorable than others, but when two individuals in the same business are in the same neighborhood and one gets rich while the other fails, it indicates that getting rich is the result of doing things in a Certain Way.

Fact #2

And further, the ability to do things in this Certain Way is not due solely to the possession of talent; many people who have great talent remain poor, while others who have very little talent get rich.

Studying the people who have gotten rich, we find that they are an average lot in all respects, having no greater talents and abilities than other people. It is evident that they do not get rich because they possess talents and abilities that other people do not have, but because they happen to do things in a Certain Way.

Fact #3

Getting rich is not the result of saving or thriftiness. Many very penurious people are poor, while free-spending spenders often get rich.

Fact #4

Nor is getting rich due to doing things which others fail to do; for two men in the same business often do almost exactly the same things, and one gets rich while the other remains poor or becomes a bankrupt. From all these things, we must come to the conclusion that getting rich is the result of doing things in a Certain Way. If getting rich is the result of doing things in a Certain Way, and if like causes always produce like effects, then any man or woman who can do things in that way can become rich, and the whole matter is brought within the domain of exact science.

The question arises here whether this Certain Way may not be so difficult that only a few may follow it. This cannot be true, as we have seen, so far as natural ability is concerned. Talented people get rich, and blockheads get rich; intellectually brilliant people get rich, and very stupid people get rich; physically strong people get rich, and weak and sickly people get rich.

Some degree of ability to think and understand is, of course, essential. But in so far as natural ability is concerned, any man or woman who has sense enough to read and understand these words can certainly get rich.

Also, we have seen that it is not a matter of environment. Location counts for something—you would not go to a hot tropical island, set up a hot chocolate stand, and expect to do successful business.

Getting rich involves the necessity of dealing with people and being where these people are. If these people are inclined to deal in the way you want to deal, so much the better. But that is about as far as environment goes.

If anybody else in your town can get rich, so can you. If anybody else in your state can get rich, so can you.

Again, it is not a matter of choosing some particular business or profession. People get rich in every business and in every profession, while their next-door neighbors in the same vocation remain in poverty.

It is true that you will do best in a business which you like and which is congenial to you. If you have certain talents which are well developed, you will do best in a business which calls for the exercise of those talents. Also, you will do best in a business which is suited to your locality; an ice cream parlor would do better in a warm climate than in Greenland, and a salmon fishery will succeed better in the Northwest than in Florida, where there are no salmon.

But, aside from these general limitations, getting rich is not dependent upon your engaging in some particular business but upon your learning to do things in a Certain Way. If you are now in business and anybody else in your locality is getting rich in the same business while you are not getting rich, it is because you are not doing things in the same Way that the other person is doing them.

Fact #5

No one is prevented from getting rich by lack of capital. True, as you get capital, the increase becomes more easy and rapid, but one who has capital is already rich and does not need to consider how to become so. No matter how poor you may be, if you begin to do things in the Certain way, you will begin to get rich, and you will begin to have capital. The getting of capital is a part of the process of getting rich, and it is a part of the result which invariably follows the doing of things in the Certain Way.

You may be the poorest man on the continent and be deeply in debt; you may have neither friends, influence, nor resources; but if you begin to do things in this Way, you must infallibly begin to get rich, for like causes must produce like effects. If you have no capital, you can get capital; if you are in the wrong business, you can get into the right business; if you are in the wrong location, you can go to the right location; and you can do so by beginning in your present business and in your present location to do things in the Certain Way which causes success.

~ 10 ~

IS OPPORTUNITY
MONOPOLIZED?

No man or woman is kept poor because opportunity has been taken away from them; because other people have monopolized the wealth and have put a fence around it. You may be shut off from engaging in business in certain lines, but there are other channels open to you. Probably it would be hard for you to get control of any of the great airlines; that field is pretty well monopolized. But the artificial intelligence business is still in its infancy and offers plenty of scope for enterprise.

It is quite true that if you work in the employ of a steel mill, you have very little chance of becoming the owner of the plant in which you work. But it is also true that if you will commence to act in a Certain Way, you can soon leave the employ of the steel mill and start your own business. There is great opportunity at this time for anyone who will think, act, and work in a Certain Way.

At different periods, the tide of opportunity sets in different directions, according to the needs of the Whole, and the particular stage of social evolution which has been reached. At present, the world, it is setting toward artificial intelligence and related industries and professions. Today, opportunity is open to the creators and users of artificial intelligence in the application of products that provide algorithms for a wide variety of services—from strategic management decisions and autopilot investing to self-driving cars.

There is abundance of opportunity for the man who will go with the tide instead of trying to swim against it.

So the factory workers, either as individuals or as a class, are not deprived of opportunity. The workers are not being "kept down" by their masters; they are not being "ground" by the trusts and combinations of capital. They are where they are because they do not do things in a Certain Way.

The working class may become the master class whenever they will begin to do things in a Certain Way; the law of wealth is the same for them as it is for all others. This they must learn, or they will remain where they are as long as they continue to do as they do. The individual worker, however, is not held down by the ignorance or the mental slothfulness of their class. They can follow the tide of opportunity to riches, and this book will tell him how.

No one is kept in poverty by a shortness in the supply of riches; there is more than enough for all. A palace as large as the capitol at Washington might be built for every family on earth from the building material in the United States alone, and under intensive cultivation, this country would produce wool, cotton, linen, and silk enough to clothe each person in the world finer than Solomon was arrayed in all his glory, together with food enough to feed them all luxuriously. The visible supply is practically inexhaustible, and the invisible supply really IS inexhaustible.

> Everything you see on earth is made from one original substance, out of which all things proceed.

New forms are constantly being made, and older ones are dissolving, but all are shapes assumed by One Thing. There is no limit to the supply of Formless Stuff, or Original Substance. The universe is made out of it, but it was not all used in making the universe. The spaces in, through, and between the forms of the visible universe are permeated and filled with the Original Substance; with the Formless Stuff; with the raw material of all things. Ten thousand times as much as has been made might still be made, and even then we should not have exhausted the supply of universal raw material.

No man, therefore, is poor because nature is poor or because there is not enough to go around. Nature is an inexhaustible storehouse of riches; the supply will never run short. Original Substance is alive with creative energy and is constantly producing more forms. When the supply of building material is exhausted, more will be produced; when the soil is exhausted so that foodstuffs and materials for clothing will no longer grow upon it, it will be renewed or more soil will be made. When all the gold and silver has been dug from the earth, if man is still in such a stage of social development that he needs gold and silver, more will be produced from the Formless. The Formless Stuff responds to the needs of man; it will not let him be without any good thing.

This is true of man collectively; the race as a whole is always abundantly rich, and if individuals are poor, it is because they do not follow the Certain Way of doing things which makes the individual man rich.

The Formless Stuff is intelligent; it is stuff which thinks. It is alive and is always impelled toward more life. It is the natural and inherent impulse of life to seek to live more; it is the nature of intelligence to enlarge itself and of consciousness to seek to extend its boundaries and find fuller expression. The universe of forms has been made by Formless Living Substance, throwing itself into form in order to express itself more fully.

The universe is a great Living Presence, always moving inherently toward more life and fuller functioning. Nature is formed for the advancement of life; its impelling motive is the increase of life. For this cause, everything which can possibly minister to life is bountifully provided; there can be no lack unless God is to contradict himself and nullify his own works.

You are not kept poor by lack in the supply of riches; it is a fact, which I shall demonstrate a little farther on, that even the resources of the Formless Supply are at the command of the man or woman who will act and think in a Certain Way.

~ 11 ~

THE FIRST PRINCIPLE IN THE
SCIENCE OF GETTING RICH

Thought is the only power which can produce tangible riches from the Formless Substance. The stuff from which all things are made is a substance which thinks, and a thought of form in this substance produces the form.

Original Substance moves according to its thoughts; every form and process you see in nature is the visible expression of a thought in Original Substance. As the Formless Stuff thinks of a form, it takes that form; as it thinks of a motion, it makes that motion. That is the way all things were created. We live in a thought world, which is part of a thought universe.

The thought of a moving universe extended throughout Formless Substance, and the Thinking Stuff moving according to that thought took the form of systems of planets and maintains that form. Thinking Substance takes the form of its thought and moves according to the thought. Holding the idea of a circling system of suns and worlds, it takes the form of these bodies and moves them as it thinks. Thinking the form of a slow-growing oak tree, it moves accordingly and produces the tree, though centuries may be required to do the work. In creating, the Formless seems to move according to the lines of motion it has established; the thought of an oak tree does not cause the instant formation of a full-grown tree, but it does start in motion the forces which will produce the tree along established lines of growth.

Every thought of form, held in thinking Substance, causes the creation of the form, but always, or at least generally, along lines of growth and action already established.

The thought of a house of a certain construction, if it were impressed upon Formless Substance, might not cause the instant formation of the house, but it would cause the turning of creative energies already working in trade and commerce into such channels as to result in the speedy building of the house. And if there were no existing channels through which the creative energy could work, then the house would be formed directly from primal substance, without waiting for the slow processes of the organic and inorganic world.

No thought of form can be impressed upon Original Substance without causing the creation of the form.

Man is a thinking center and can originate thought. All the forms that man fashions with his hands must first exist in his thought; he cannot shape a thing until he has thought that thing.

And so far, man has confined his efforts wholly to the work of his hands; he has applied manual labor to the world of forms, seeking to change or modify those already existing. He has never thought of trying to cause the creation of new forms by impressing his thoughts upon Formless Substance.

When man has a thought form, he takes material from the forms of nature and makes an image of the form which is in his mind. He has, so far, made little or no effort to co-operate with Formless Intelligence; to work "with the Father." He has not dreamed that he can "do what he seeth the Father doing." Man re-shapes and modifies existing forms by manual labor; he has given no attention to the question whether he may not produce things from Formless Substance by communicating his thoughts to it. We propose to prove that he may do so, to prove that any man or woman may do so, and to show how. As our first step, we must lay down three fundamental propositions.

First, we assert that there is one original formless stuff, or substance, from which all things are made. All the seemingly many elements are but different presentations of one element; all the many forms found in organic and inorganic nature are but different shapes made from the same stuff. And this stuff is thinking stuff; a thought held in it produces the form of the thought. Thought, in thinking substance, produces shapes. Man is a thinking center capable of original thought; if man can communicate his thought to original thinking substance, he can cause the creation, or formation, of the thing he thinks about. To summarize this:

- There is a thinking stuff from which all things are made and which, in its original state, permeates, penetrates, and fills the interspaces of the universe.
- A thought, in this substance, produces the thing that is imaged by the thought.
- Man can form things in his thought, and, by impressing his thought upon formless substance, can cause the thing he thinks about to be created.

It may be asked if I can prove these statements, and without going into details, I answer that I can do so, both by logic and experience.

Reasoning back from the phenomena of form and thought, I come to one original thinking substance, and reasoning forward from this thinking substance, I come to man's power to cause the formation of the thing he thinks about.

And by experiment, I find the reasoning true, and this is my strongest proof.

If one man who reads this book gets rich by doing what it tells him to do, that is evidence in support of my claim; but if every man who does what it tells him to do gets rich, that is positive proof until some one goes through the process and fails. The theory is true until the process fails, and this process will not fail, for every man who does exactly what this book tells him to do will get rich.

I have said that men get rich by doing things in a Certain Way; and in order to do so, men must become able to think in a certain way.

> A man's way of doing things is the direct result of the way he thinks about things.

To do things in the way you want to do them, you will have to acquire the ability to think the way you want to think; this is the first step toward getting rich. To think what you want to think is to think TRUTH, regardless of appearances.

Every man has the natural and inherent power to think what he wants to think, but it requires far more effort to do so than it does to think the thoughts which are suggested by appearances. To think according to appearances is easy; to think truth regardless of appearances is laborious and requires the expenditure of more power than any other work man is called upon to perform.

There is no labor from which most people shrink as they do from that of sustained and consecutive thought; it is the hardest work in the world. This is especially true when truth is contrary to appearances. Every appearance in the visible world tends to produce a corresponding form in the mind which observes it, and this can only be prevented by holding the thought of the TRUTH.

~ 12 ~

INCREASING LIFE

You must get rid of the last vestige of the old idea that there is a Deity whose will it is that you should be poor or whose purposes may be served by keeping you in poverty. The Intelligent substance, which is All, and in all and which lives in All and lives in you, is a consciously Living Substance. Being a consciously living substance, It must have the natural and inherent desire of every living intelligence for increase of life. Every living thing must continually seek for the enlargement of its life, because life, in the mere act of living, must increase itself.

A seed dropped into the ground springs into activity, and in the act of living produces a hundred more seeds; life, by living, multiplies itself. It is forever Becoming More; it must do so if it continues to be at all.

Intelligence is under this same necessity for continuous increase. Every thought we think makes it necessary for us to think another thought; consciousness is continually expanding. Every fact we learn leads us to the learning of another fact; knowledge is continually increasing. Every talent we cultivate brings to the mind the desire to cultivate another talent; we are subject to the urge of life, seeking expression, which ever drives us on to know more, to do more, and to be more.

In order to know more, do more, and be more, we must have more; we must have things to use, for we learn, and do, and become only by using things. We must get rich so that we can live more.

The desire for riches is simply the capacity for larger life seeking fulfillment; every desire is the effort of an unexpressed possibility to come into action. It is power seeking to manifest which causes desire. That which makes you want more money is the same as that which makes the plant grow; it is Life, seeking fuller expression.

The One Living Substance must be subject to this inherent law of all life; it is permeated with the desire to live more, that is why it is under the necessity of creating things. The One Substance desires to live more in you; hence, it wants you to have all the things you can use. It is the desire of God that you should get rich. He wants you to get rich because he can express himself better through you if you have plenty of things to use in giving him expression. He can live more in you if you have unlimited command of the means of life.

The universe desires you to have everything you want. Nature is friendly to your plans. Everything is naturally for you. Make up your mind that this is true. It is essential, however, that your purpose should harmonize with the purpose that is in All. You must want real life, not mere pleasure or sensual gratification. Life is the performance of function; and the individual really lives only when he performs every function, physical, mental, and spiritual, of which he is capable, without excess in any.

You do not want to get rich in order to live swinishly for the gratification of animal desires; that is not life. But the performance of every physical function is a part of life, and no one lives completely who denies the impulses of the body a normal and healthful expression.

You do not want to get rich solely to enjoy mental pleasures, to get knowledge, to gratify ambition, to outshine others, to be famous. All these are a legitimate part of life, but the man who lives for the pleasures of the intellect alone will only have a partial life, and he will never be satisfied with his lot.

You do not want to get rich solely for the good of others, to lose yourself for the salvation of mankind, to experience the joys of philanthropy and sacrifice. The joys of the soul are only a part of life, and they are no better or nobler than any other part.

You want to get rich in order that you may eat, drink, and be merry when it is time to do these things; in order that you may surround yourself with beautiful things, see distant lands, feed your mind, and develop your intellect; in order that you may love men, do kind things, and be able to play a good part in helping the world to find truth. But remember that extreme altruism is no better and no nobler than extreme selfishness; both are mistakes.

Get rid of the idea that God wants you to sacrifice yourself for others and that you can secure his favor by doing so; God requires nothing of the kind.

What he wants is that you should make the most of yourself, for yourself and for others, and you can help others more by making the most of yourself than in any other way. You can make the most of yourself only by getting rich, so it is right and praiseworthy that you should give your first and best thought to the work of acquiring wealth.

Remember, however, that the desire of Substance is for all, and its movements must be for more life to all; it cannot be made to work for less life to any because it is equally in all, seeking riches and life.

Intelligent Substance will make things for you, but it will not take things away from someone else and give them to you.

You must get rid of the thought of competition. You are to create, not to compete for what is already created. You do not have to take anything away from any one. You do not have to drive sharp bargains. You do not have to cheat or to take advantage. You do not need to let any man work for you for less than he earns. You do not have to covet the property of others or to look at it with wishful eyes; no man has anything of which you cannot have the like, and that without taking what he has away from him. You are to become a creator, not a competitor; you are going to get what you want, but in such a way that when you get it, every other man will have more than he has now.

I am aware that there are men who get a vast amount of money by proceeding in direct opposition to the statements in the paragraph above, and may add a word of explanation here. Men of the plutocratic type who become very rich do so sometimes purely by their extraordinary ability on the plane of competition, and sometimes they unconsciously relate themselves to Substance in its great purposes and movements for the general racial upbuilding through industrial evolution. Rockefeller, Carnegie, Morgan, et all have been the unconscious agents of the Supreme in the necessary work of systematizing and organizing productive industry, and in the end, their work will contribute immensely toward increased life for all. Their day is nearly over; they have organized production and will soon be succeeded by the agents of the multitude, who will organize the machinery of distribution. The multi-millionaires are like the monster reptiles of the prehistoric eras; they play a necessary part in the evolutionary process, but the same Power which produced them will dispose of them. And it is well to bear in mind that they have never been really rich; a record of the private lives of most of this class will show that they have really been the most abject and wretched of the poor.

Riches secured on the competitive plane are never satisfactory and permanent; they are yours today and another's tomorrow. Remember, if you are to become rich in a scientific and certain way, you must rise entirely out of the competitive thought. You must never think for a moment that the supply is limited. Just as soon as you begin to think that all the money is being "cornered" and controlled by bankers and others and that you must exert yourself to get laws passed to stop this process, and so on, in that moment you drop into the competitive mind, and your power to cause creation is gone for the time being; and what is worse, you will probably arrest the creative movements you have already instituted.

KNOW that there are countless millions of dollars' worth of gold in the mountains of the earth, not yet brought to light, and know that if there were not, more would be created from Thinking Substance to supply your needs.

KNOW that the money you need will come, even if it is necessary for a thousand men to be led to the discovery of new gold mines to-morrow.

Never look at the visible supply; look always at the limitless riches in Formless Substance, and KNOW that they are coming to you as fast as you can receive and use them. Nobody, by cornering the visible supply, can prevent you from getting what is yours.

So never allow yourself to think for an instant that all the best building spots will be taken before you get ready to build your house, unless you hurry. Never worry about the trusts and combines, and get anxious for fear they will soon come to own the whole earth. Never get afraid that you will lose what you want because some other person "beats you to it." That cannot possibly happen; you are not seeking anything that is possessed by anybody else; you are causing what you want to be created from Formless Substance, and the supply is without limits. Stick to the formulated statement: There is a thinking stuff from which all things are made and which, in its original state, permeates, penetrates, and fills the interspaces of the universe. A thought, in this substance, produces the thing that is imaged by the thought. Man can form things in his thought, and, by impressing his thought upon formless substance, can cause the thing he thinks about to be created.

~ 13 ~

HOW RICHES COME TO YOU

When I say that you do not have to drive sharp bargains, I do not mean that you do not have to drive any bargains at all or that you are above the necessity for having any dealings with your fellow men. I mean that you will not need to deal with them unfairly; you do not have to get something for nothing, but can give to every man more than you take from him.

You cannot give every man more in cash market value than you take from him, but you can give him more in use value than the cash value of the thing you take from him. The paper, ink, and other material in this book may not be worth the money you paid for it, but if the ideas suggested by it bring you thousands of dollars, you have not been wronged by those who sold it to you; they have given you a great use value for a small cash value.

Let us suppose that I own a picture by one of the great artists, which, in any civilized community, is worth thousands of dollars. I take it to Baffin Bay and, by salesmanship," induce an Eskimo to give a bundle of furs worth $500 for it. I have really wronged him, for he has no use for the picture; it has no use value to him; it will not add to his life.

But suppose I give him a gun worth $50 for his furs; then he has made a good bargain. He has use for the gun; it will get him many more furs and much food; it will add to his life in every way; it will make him rich.

When you rise from the competitive to the creative plane, you can scan your business transactions very strictly, and if you are selling any man anything which does not add more to his life than the thing he gives you in exchange, you can afford to stop it. You do not have to beat anybody in business. And if you are in a business which does beat people, get out of it at once.

Give every man more in use value than you take from him in cash value; then you are adding to the life of the world by every business transaction.

If you have people working for you, you must take from them more in cash value than you pay them in wages, but you can so organize your business that it will be filled with the principle of advancement and so that each employee who wishes to do so may advance a little every day.

You can make your business do for your employees what this book is doing for you. You can so conduct your business that it will be a sort of ladder by which every employee who will take the trouble may climb to riches himself, and given the opportunity, if he will not do so, it is not your fault.

And finally, because you are to cause the creation of your riches from Formless Substance which permeates all your environment, it does not follow that they are to take shape from the atmosphere and come into being before your eyes.

If you want a sewing machine, for instance, I do not mean to tell you that you are to impress the thought of a sewing machine on Thinking Substance until the machine is formed without hands, in the room where you sit, or elsewhere. But if you want a sewing machine, hold the mental image of it with the most positive certainty that it is being made or is on its way to you. After once forming the thought, have the most absolute and unquestioning faith that the sewing machine is coming; never think of it or speak of it in any other way than as being sure to arrive. Claim it as already yours.

It will be brought to you by the power of the Supreme Intelligence, acting upon the minds of men. If you live in Maine, it may be that a man will be brought from Texas or Japan to engage in some transaction which will result in your getting what you want. If so, the whole matter will be as much to that man's advantage as it is to yours.

Do not forget for a moment that the Thinking Substance is through all, in all, communicating with all, and can influence all. The desire of Thinking Substance for fuller life and better living has caused the creation of all the sewing machines already made, and it can cause the creation of millions more and will, whenever men set it in motion by desire and faith and by acting in a Certain Way.

You can certainly have a sewing machine in your house, and it is just as certain that you can have any other thing or things which you want and which you will use for the advancement of your own life and the lives of others.

You need not hesitate about asking largely; "it is your Father's pleasure to give you the kingdom," said Jesus. Original Substance wants to live all that is possible in you and wants you to have all that you can or will use for the living of the most abundant life. If you fix upon your consciousness the fact that the desire you feel for the possession of riches is one with the desire of Omnipotence for more complete expression, your faith becomes invincible.

Once I saw a little boy sitting at a piano and vainly trying to bring harmony out of the keys, and I saw that he was grieved and provoked by his inability to play real music. I asked him the cause of his vexation, and he answered, "I can feel the music in me, but I can't make my hands go right." The music in him was the URGE of Original Substance, containing all the possibilities of all life; all that there is of music was seeking expression through the child.

God, the One Substance, is trying to live, do, and enjoy things through humanity. He is saying, "I want hands to build wonderful structures, to play divine harmonies, to paint glorious pictures; I want feet to run my errands; eyes to see my beauties; tongues to tell mighty truths and to sing marvelous songs," and so on.

All that there is of possibility is seeking expression through men. God wants those who can play music to have pianos and every other instrument and to have the means to cultivate their talents to the fullest extent; He wants those who can appreciate beauty to be able to surround themselves with beautiful things; He wants those who can discern truth to have every opportunity to travel and observe; He wants those who can appreciate dress to be beautifully clothed; and those who can appreciate good food to be luxuriously fed.

He wants all these things because it is Himself that enjoys and appreciates them; it is God who wants to play, and sing, and enjoy beauty, and proclaim truth, and wear fine clothes, and eat good foods. "It is God that works in you to will and to do," said Paul. The desire you feel for riches is the Infinite, seeking to express Himself in you as He sought to find expression in the little boy at the piano. So you need not hesitate to ask largely.

Your part is to focalize and express the desires of God. This is a difficult point with most people; they retain something of the old idea that poverty and self-sacrifice are pleasing to God. They look upon poverty as a part of the plan, a necessity of nature. They have the idea that God has finished His work and made all that He can make, and that the majority of men must stay poor because there is not enough to go around. They hold to so much of this erroneous thought that they feel ashamed to ask for wealth; they try not to want more than a very modest competence, just enough to make them fairly comfortable.

I recall now the case of one student who was told that he must get in mind a clear picture of the things he desired so that the creative thought of them might be impressed on Formless Substance. He was a very poor man, living in a rented house and having only what he earned from day to day, and he could not grasp the fact that all wealth was his. So, after thinking the matter over, he decided that he might reasonably ask for a new rug for the floor of his best room and an anthracite coal stove to heat the house during the cold weather. Following the instructions given in this book, he obtained these things in a few months, and then it dawned upon him that he had not asked enough. He went through the house in which he lived and planned all the improvements he would like to make in it; he mentally added a bay window here and a room there until it was complete in his mind as his ideal home; and then he planned its furnishings.

Holding the whole picture in his mind, he began living in the Certain Way, and moving toward what he wanted, and he owns the house now, and is rebuilding it after the form of his mental image. And now, with still larger faith, he is going on to get greater things. It has been unto him according to his faith, and it is so with you and with all of us.

~ 14 ~

GRATITUDE.

The illustrations given in the last chapter will have conveyed to the reader the fact that the first step toward getting rich is to convey the idea of your wants to the Formless Substance.

This is true, and you will see that in order to do so, it becomes necessary to relate yourself to the Formless Intelligence in a harmonious way.

To secure this harmonious relation is a matter of such primary and vital importance that I shall give some space to its discussion here and give you instructions which, if you will follow them, will be certain to bring you into perfect unity of mind with God.

The whole process of mental adjustment and atonement can be summed up in one word: gratitude.

First, you believe that there is one Intelligent Substance, from which all things proceed; second, you believe that this Substance gives you everything you desire; and third, you relate yourself to It by a feeling of deep and profound gratitude. Many people who order their lives rightly in all other ways are kept in poverty by their lack of gratitude. Having received one gift from God, they cut the wires which connect them with Him by failing to make acknowledgment.

It is easy to understand that the nearer we live to the source of wealth, the more wealth we shall receive, and it is easy also to understand that the soul that is always grateful lives in closer touch with God than the one which never looks to Him in thankful acknowledgment.

The more gratefully we fix our minds on the Supreme when good things come to us, the more good things we will receive and the more rapidly they will come, and the reason simply is that the mental attitude of gratitude draws the mind into closer touch with the source from which the blessings come.

If it is a new thought to you that gratitude brings your whole mind into closer harmony with the creative energies of the universe, consider it well, and you will see that it is true. The good things you already have come to you along the line of obedience to certain laws. Gratitude will lead your mind out along the ways by which things come, and it will keep you in close harmony with creative thought and prevent you from falling into competitive thought.

Gratitude alone can keep you looking toward the All and prevent you from falling into the error of thinking of the supply as limited, and to do that would be fatal to your hopes. There is a Law of Gratitude, and it is absolutely necessary that you should observe the law, if you are to get the results you seek. The law of gratitude is the natural principle that action and reaction are always equal and in opposite directions.

The grateful outreaching of your mind in thankful praise to the Supreme is a liberation or expenditure of force; it cannot fail to reach that to which it is addressed, and the reaction is an instantaneous movement toward you.

"Draw nigh unto God, and He will draw nigh unto you." That is a statement of psychological truth. And if your gratitude is strong and constant, the reaction in Formless Substance will be strong and continuous; the movement of the things you want will be always toward you. Notice the grateful attitude that Jesus took; how He always seems to be saying, "I thank Thee, Father, that Thou hearest me." You cannot exercise much power without gratitude, for it is gratitude that keeps you connected with Power. But the value of gratitude does not consist solely in getting you more blessings in the future. Without gratitude, you cannot long keep from dissatisfied thought regarding things as they are.

The moment you permit your mind to dwell with dissatisfaction upon things as they are, you begin to lose ground. You fix attention upon the common, the ordinary, the poor, and the squalid and mean, and your mind takes the form of these things. Then you will transmit these forms or mental images to the Formless, and the common, the poor, the squalid, and mean will come to you. To permit your mind to dwell upon the inferior is to become inferior and to surround yourself with inferior things. On the other hand, to fix your attention on the best, is to surround yourself with the best and to become the best.

The Creative Power within us makes us into the image of that to which we give our attention. We are Thinking Substance, and thinking substance always takes the form of that which it thinks about. The grateful mind is constantly fixed upon the best; therefore, it tends to become the best; it takes the form or character of the best and will receive the best.

Also, faith is born of gratitude. The grateful mind continually expects good things, and expectation becomes faith. The reaction of gratitude upon one's own mind produces faith, and every outgoing wave of grateful thanksgiving increases faith. He who has no feeling of gratitude cannot long retain a living faith, and without a living faith, you cannot get rich by the creative method, as we shall see in the following chapters.

It is necessary, then, to cultivate the habit of being grateful for every good thing that comes to you and to give thanks continuously. And because all things have contributed to your advancement, you should include all things in your gratitude. Do not waste time thinking or talking about the shortcomings or wrong actions of plutocrats or trust magnates. Their organization of the world has made your opportunity; all you get really comes to you because of them. Do not rage against corrupt politicians; if it were not for politicians, we should fall into anarchy, and your opportunity would be greatly lessened.

God has worked a long time and very patiently to bring us up to where we are in industry and government, and He is going right on with His work. There is not the least doubt that He will do away with plutocrats, trust magnates, captains of industry, and politicians as soon as they can be spared; but in the meantime, behold, they are all very good. Remember that they are all helping to arrange the lines of transmission along which your riches will come to you, and be grateful to them all. This will bring you into harmonious relations with the good in everything, and the good in everything will move toward you.

~ 15 ~

THINKING IN THE CERTAIN WAY

Turn back to chapter VI and read again the story of the man who formed a mental image of his house, and you will get a fair idea of the initial step toward getting rich. You must form a clear and definite mental picture of what you want; you cannot transmit an idea unless you have it yourself.

You must have it before you can give it, and many people fail to impress Thinking Substance because they have themselves only a vague and misty concept of the things they want to do, to have, or to become.

It is not enough that you should have a general desire for wealth "to do good with"; everybody has that desire. It is not enough that you should have a wish to travel, see things, live more, etc. Everybody has those desires, also. If you were going to send a wireless message to a friend, you would not send the letters of the alphabet in their order and let him construct the message for himself, nor would you take words at random from the dictionary. You would send a coherent sentence, one which meant something. When you try to impress your wants upon Substance, remember that it must be done by a coherent statement; you must know what you want and be definite.

You can never get rich or start the creative power into action by sending out unformed longings and vague desires. Go over your desires just as the man I have described went over his house; see just what you want, and get a clear mental picture of it as you wish it to look when you get it. That clear mental picture you must have continually in mind, as the sailor has in mind the port toward which he is sailing the ship; you must keep your face toward it all the time. You must no more lose sight of it than the steersman loses sight of the compass.

It is not necessary to take exercises in concentration, nor to set apart special times for prayer and affirmation, nor to "go into the silence," nor to do occult stunts of any kind. These things are well enough, but all you need is to know what you want and to want it badly enough so that it will stay in your thoughts. Spend as much of your leisure time as you can in contemplating your picture, but no one needs to take exercises to concentrate his mind on a thing which he really wants; it is the things you do not really care about which require effort to fix your attention upon them.

And unless you really want to get rich, so that the desire is strong enough to hold your thoughts directed to the purpose as the magnetic pole holds the needle of the compass, it will hardly be worth while for you to try to carry out the instructions given in this book.

The methods herein set forth are for people whose desire for riches is strong enough to overcome mental laziness and the love of ease and make them work. The more clear and definite you make your picture, then, and the more you dwell upon it, bringing out all its delightful details, the stronger your desire will be, and the stronger your desire, the easier it will be to hold your mind fixed upon the picture of what you want.

Something more is necessary, however, than merely to see the picture clearly. If that is all you do, you are only a dreamer and will have little or no power for accomplishment. Behind your clear vision must be the purpose to realize it—to bring it out in tangible expression.

And behind this purpose must be an invincible and unwavering FAITH that the thing is already yours; that it is "at hand" and you have only to take possession of it.

Live in the new house mentally until it takes form around you physically. In the mental realm, enter at once into full enjoyment of the things you want. "Whatsoever things ye ask for when ye pray, believe that ye receive them, and ye shall have them," said Jesus. See the things you want as if they were actually around you all the time; see yourself as owning and using them. Make use of them in imagination just as you will use them when they are your tangible possessions. Dwell upon your mental picture until it is clear and distinct, and then take the Mental Attitude of Ownership toward everything in that picture. Take possession of it in mind, in the full faith that it is actually yours. Hold to this mental ownership; do not waver for an instant in the faith that it is real.

And remember what was said in the preceding chapter about gratitude: be as thankful for it all the time as you expect to be when it has taken form. The man who can sincerely thank God for the things which as yet, he owns only in imagination has real faith. He will get rich; he will cause the creation of whatsoever he wants. You do not need to pray repeatedly for the things you want; it is not necessary to tell God about it every day. "Use not vain repetitions as the heathen do," said Jesus to His pupils, "for your Father knows that you have need of these things before ye ask Him." Your part is to intelligently formulate your desire for the things which make for a larger life, and to get these desires arranged into a coherent whole, and then to impress this Whole Desire upon the Formless Substance, which has the power and the will to bring you what you want.

You do not make this impression by repeating strings of words; you make it by holding the vision with unshakable PURPOSE to attain it and with steadfast FAITH that you do attain it. The answer to prayer is not according to your faith while you are talking, but according to your faith while you are working. You cannot impress the mind of God by having a special Sabbath day set apart to tell Him what you want and then forgetting Him during the rest of the week. You cannot impress Him by having special hours to go into your closet and pray if you then dismiss the matter from your mind until the hour of prayer comes again.

Oral prayer is well enough and has its effect, especially upon yourself, in clarifying your vision and strengthening your faith, but it is not your oral petitions which get you what you want. In order to get rich, you do not need a "sweet hour of prayer"; you need to "pray without ceasing." And by prayer, I mean holding steadily to your vision with the purpose to cause its creation into solid form and the faith that you are doing so:

Believe that ye receive them.

The whole matter turns on receiving once you have clearly formed your vision. When you have formed it, it is well to make an oral statement, addressing the Supreme in reverent prayer, and from that moment on, you must, in mind, receive what you ask for. Live in the new house; wear the fine clothes; ride in the automobile; go on the journey; and confidently plan for greater journeys. Think and speak of all the things you have asked for in terms of actual present ownership. Imagine an environment and a financial condition exactly as you want them, and live all the time in that imaginary environment and financial condition. Mind, however, that you do not do this as a mere dreamer and castle builder; hold to the FAITH that the imaginary is being realized and to the PURPOSE to realize it. Remember that it is faith and purpose in the use of the imagination which make the difference between the scientist and the dreamer. And having learned this fact, it is here that you must learn the proper use of the Will.

~ 16 ~

HOW TO USE THE WILL

To set about getting rich in a scientific way, you do not try to apply your will power to anything outside of yourself. You have no right to do so anyway.

It is wrong to apply your will to other men and women in order to get them to do what you wish. It is as flagrantly wrong to coerce people by mental power as it is to coerce them by physical power. If compelling people by physical force to do things for you reduces them to slavery, compelling them by mental means accomplishes exactly the same thing; the only difference is in methods. If taking things from people by physical force is robbery, then taking things by mental force is robbery also; there is no difference in principle. You have no right to use your will power upon another person, even "for his own good"; for you do not know what is for his good.

The science of getting rich does not require you to apply power or force to any other person in any way whatsoever. There is not the slightest necessity for doing so; indeed, any attempt to use your will upon others will only tend to defeat your purpose. You do not need to apply your will to things in order to compel them to come to you.

That would simply be trying to coerce God and would be foolish, useless, as well as irreverent. You do not have to compel God to give you good things any more than you have to use your will power to make the sun rise. You do not have to use your will power to conquer an unfriendly deity or to make stubborn and rebellious forces do your bidding.

Substance is friendly to you and is more anxious to give you what you want than you are to get it. To get rich, you need only to use your will power upon yourself. When you know what to think and do, then you must use your will to compel yourself to think and do the right things. That is the legitimate use of the will in getting what you want—to use it in holding yourself to the right course. Use your will to keep yourself thinking and acting in the Certain Way.

Do not try to project your will, or your thoughts, or your mind out into space to "act" on things or people. Keep your mind at home; it can accomplish more there than elsewhere. Use your mind to form a mental image of what you want and to hold that vision with faith and purpose; and use your will to keep your mind working in the Right Way. The more steady and continuous your faith and purpose, the more rapidly you will get rich, because you will make only POSITIVE impressions upon Substance; and you will not neutralize or offset them by negative impressions.

The picture of your desires, held with faith and purpose, is taken up by the Formless, and permeates it to great distances,—throughout the universe, for all I know. As this impression spreads, all things are set moving toward its realization: every living thing, every inanimate thing, and the things yet uncreated are stirred toward bringing into being that which you want. All force begins to be exerted in that direction; all things begin to move toward you. The minds of people everywhere are influenced toward doing the things necessary to the fulfilling of your desires, and they work for you unconsciously.

But you can check all this by starting a negative impression in the Formless Substance. Doubt or unbelief is as certain to start a movement away from you as faith and purpose are to start one toward you. It is by not understanding this that most people who try to make use of "mental science" in getting rich make their failure.

Every hour and moment you spend in giving heed to doubts and fears, every hour you spend in worry, every hour in which your soul is possessed by unbelief, sets a current away from you in the whole domain of intelligent Substance. All the promises are unto them that believe, and unto them only. Notice how insistent Jesus was upon this point of belief, and now you know the reason why.

Since belief is all-important, it behooves you to guard your thoughts, and as your beliefs will be shaped to a very great extent by the things you observe and think about, it is important that you should command your attention. And here the will comes into use, for it is by your will that you determine upon what things your attention shall be fixed. If you want to become rich, you must not make a study of poverty. Things are not brought into being by thinking about their opposites. Health is never to be attained by studying disease and thinking about disease; righteousness is not to be promoted by studying sin and thinking about sin; and no one ever got rich by studying poverty and thinking about poverty.

Medicine as a science of disease has increased disease; religion as a science of sin has promoted sin; and economics as a study of poverty will fill the world with wretchedness and want.

Do not talk about poverty; do not investigate it or concern yourself with it. Never mind what its causes are; you have nothing to do with them. What concerns you is the cure.

Do not spend your time in charitable work or charity movements; all charity only tends to perpetuate the wretchedness it aims to eradicate. I do not say that you should be hard-hearted or unkind and refuse to hear the cry of need, but you must not try to eradicate poverty in any of the conventional ways. Put poverty behind you and put all that pertains to it behind you, and "make good."

Get rich; that is the best way you can help the poor. And you cannot hold the mental image which is to make you rich if you fill your mind with pictures of poverty. Do not read books or papers which give circumstantial accounts of the wretchedness of the tenement dwellers, of the horrors of child labor, and so on. Do not read anything which fills your mind with gloomy images of want and suffering.

You cannot help the poor in the least by knowing about these things, and the wide-spread knowledge of them does not tend at all to do away with poverty. What tends to do away with poverty is not the getting of pictures of poverty into your mind but getting pictures of wealth into the minds of the poor. You are not deserting the poor in their misery when you refuse to allow your mind to be filled with pictures of that misery.

Poverty can be done away with not by increasing the number of well-to-do people who think about poverty but by increasing the number of poor people who propose with faith to get rich. The poor do not need charity; they need inspiration. Charity only sends them a loaf of bread to keep them alive in their wretchedness or gives them an entertainment to make them forget for an hour or two, but inspiration will cause them to rise out of their misery. If you want to help the poor, demonstrate to them that they can become rich; prove it by getting rich yourself.

The only way in which poverty will ever be banished from this world is by getting a large and constantly increasing number of people to practice the teachings of this book. People must be taught to become rich by creation, not by competition. Every man who becomes rich by competition throws down behind him the ladder by which he rises and keeps others down; but every man who gets rich by creation opens a way for thousands to follow him and inspires them to do so.

You are not showing hardness of heart or an unfeeling disposition when you refuse to pity poverty, see poverty, read about poverty, or think or talk about it, or to listen to those who do talk about it. Use your will power to keep your mind OFF the subject of poverty and to keep it fixed with faith and purpose ON the vision of what you want.

~ 17 ~

FURTHER USE OF THE WILL

You cannot retain a true and clear vision of wealth if you are constantly turning your attention to opposing pictures, whether they be external or imaginary. Do not tell of your past troubles of a financial nature, if you have had them; do not think of them at all. Do not tell of the poverty of your parents or the hardships of your early life; to do any of these things is to mentally class yourself with the poor for the time being, and it will certainly check the movement of things in your direction. "Let the dead bury their dead," as Jesus said.

Put poverty and all things that pertain to poverty completely behind you. You have accepted a certain theory of the universe as being correct and are resting all your hopes of happiness on its being correct; and what can you gain by giving heed to conflicting theories? Do not read religious books which tell you that the world is soon coming to an end, and do not read the writings of muck-rakers and pessimistic philosophers who tell you that it is going to the devil. The world is not going to the devil; it is going to God. It is a wonderful Becoming.

True, there may be a good many things in existing conditions which are disagreeable, but what is the use of studying them when they are certainly passing away and when the study of them only tends to check their passing and keep them with us? Why give time and attention to things which are being removed by evolutionary growth when you can hasten their removal only by promoting the evolutionary growth as far as your part of it goes?

No matter how horrible in seeming may be the conditions in certain countries, sections, or places, you waste your time and destroy your own chances by considering them. You should interest yourself in the world's becoming rich. Think of the riches the world is coming into instead of the poverty it is growing out of, and bear in mind that the only way in which you can assist the world in growing rich is by growing rich yourself through the creative method—not the competitive one. Give your attention wholly to riches; ignore poverty.

Whenever you think or speak of those who are poor, think and speak of them as those who are becoming rich, as those who are to be congratulated rather than pitied. Then they and others will catch the inspiration and begin to search for the way out. Because I say that you are to give your whole time, mind, and thought to riches, it does not follow that you are to be sordid or mean. To become really rich is the noblest aim you can have in life, for it includes everything else. On the competitive plane, the struggle to get rich is a Godless scramble for power over other men, but when we come into the creative mind, all this is changed.

All that is possible in the way of greatness and soul unfoldment, of service and lofty endeavor, comes by way of getting rich; all is made possible by the use of things.

If you lack for physical health, you will find that the attainment of it is conditional on your getting rich. Only those who are emancipated from financial worry and who have the means to live a care-free existence and follow hygienic practices can have and retain health.

Moral and spiritual greatness is possible only to those who are above the competitive battle for existence, and only those who are becoming rich on the plane of creative thought are free from the degrading influences of competition. If your heart is set on domestic happiness, remember that love flourishes best where there is re-finement, a high level of thought, and freedom from corrupting influences, and these are to be found only where riches are attained by the exercise of creative thought, without strife or rivalry.

You can aim at nothing so great or noble, I repeat, as to become rich, and you must fix your attention upon your mental picture of riches to the exclusion of all that may tend to dim or obscure the vision.

You must learn to see the underlying TRUTH in all things; you must see beneath all seemingly wrong conditions the Great One Life ever moving forward toward fuller expression and more complete happiness.

It is the truth that there is no such thing as poverty; that there is only wealth. Some people remain in poverty because they are ignorant of the fact that there is wealth for them, and these can best be taught by showing them the way to affluence in your own person and practice.

Others are poor because, while they feel that there is a way out, they are too intellectually indolent to put forth the mental effort necessary to find that way and travel it, and for these, the very best thing you can do is to arouse their desire by showing them the happiness that comes from being rightly rich.

Others still are poor because, while they have some notion of science, they have become so swamped and lost in the maze of metaphysical and occult theories that they do not know which road to take. They try a mixture of many systems and fail in all. For these, again, the very best thing to do is to show the right way in your own person and practice; an ounce of doing things is worth a pound of theorizing. The very best thing you can do for the whole world is to make the most of yourself.

You can serve God and man in no more effective way than by getting rich; that is, if you get rich by the creative method and not by the competitive one. Another thing, we assert that this book gives in detail the principles of the science of getting rich, and if that is true, you do not need to read any other book upon the subject. This may sound narrow and egotistical, but consider: there is no more scientific method of computation in mathematics than by addition, subtraction, multiplication, and division; no other method is possible. There can be but one shortest distance between two points. There is only one way to think scientifically, and that is to think in the way that leads by the most direct and simple route to the goal. No man has yet formulated a briefer or less complex "system" than the one set forth herein; it has been stripped of all non-essentials. When you commence on this, lay all others aside; put them out of your mind altogether.

Read this book every day; keep it with you; commit it to memory; and do not think about other "systems" and theories. If you do, you will begin to have doubts and to be uncertain and wavering in your thought; and then you will begin to make failures. After you have made good and become rich, you may study other systems as much as you please, but until you are quite sure that you have gained what you want, do not read anything on this line but this book, unless it be the authors mentioned in the Preface.

And read only the most optimistic comments on the world's news—those in harmony with your picture. Also, postpone your investigations into the occult. Do not dabble in Theosophy, Spiritualism, or kindred studies. It is very likely that the dead still live and are near, but if they are, let them alone; mind your own business. Wherever the spirits of the dead may be, they have their own work to do and their own problems to solve, and we have no right to interfere with them. We cannot help them, and it is very doubtful whether they can help us or whether we have any right to trespass upon their time if they can. Let the dead and the hereafter alone, and solve your own problem; get rich. If you begin to mix with the occult, you will start mental cross-currents, which will surely bring your hopes to shipwreck. Now, this and the preceding chapters have brought us to the following statement of basic facts:

- There is a thinking stuff from which all things are made and which, in its original state, permeates, penetrates, and fills the interspaces of the universe.
- A thought, in this substance, produces the thing that is imaged by the thought.
- Man can form things in his thought, and, by impressing his thought upon formless substance, can cause the thing he thinks about to be created.
- In order to do this, man must pass from the competitive to the creative mind.
- He must form a clear mental picture of the things he wants and hold this picture in his thoughts with the fixed PURPOSE to get what he wants and the unwavering FAITH that he does get what he wants, closing his mind against all that may tend to shake his purpose, dim his vision, or quench his faith.

In addition to all this, we shall now see that he must live and act in a Certain Way.

~ 18 ~

ACTING IN A CERTAIN WAY

Thought is the creative power, or the impelling force which causes the creative power to act; thinking in a Certain Way will bring riches to you, but you must not rely upon thought alone, paying no attention to personal action. That is the rock upon which many otherwise scientific metaphysical thinkers meet shipwreck—the failure to connect thought with personal action.

We have not yet reached the stage of development, even supposing such a stage to be possible, in which man can create directly from Formless Substance without nature's processes or the work of human hands; man must not only think, but his personal action must supplement his thought.

By thought, you can cause the gold in the hearts of the mountains to be impelled toward you, but it will not mine itself, refine itself, coin itself into double eagles, and come rolling along the roads seeking its way into your pocket.

Under the impelling power of the Supreme Spirit, men's affairs will be so ordered that someone will be led to mine the gold for you; other men's business transactions will be so directed that the gold will be brought toward you; and you must so arrange your own business affairs that you may be able to receive it when it comes to you. Your thought makes all things, animate and inanimate, work to bring you what you want, but your personal activity must be such that you can rightly receive what you want when it reaches you. You are not to take it as charity nor to steal it; you must give every man more in use value than he gives you in cash value.

The scientific use of thought consists in forming a clear and distinct mental image of what you want, holding fast to the purpose to get what you want, and in realizing with grateful faith that you do get what you want.

Do not try to "project" your thought in any mysterious or occult way with the idea of having it go out and do things for you; that is wasted effort and will weaken your power to think with sanity.

The action of thought in getting rich is fully explained in the preceding chapters; your faith and purpose positively impress your vision upon Formless Substance, which has THE SAME DESIRE FOR MORE LIFE THAT YOU HAVE; and this vision, received from you, sets all the creative forces at work IN AND THROUGH THEIR REGU-LAR CHANNELS OF ACTION, but directed toward you.

It is not your part to guide or supervise the creative process; all you have to do with that is to retain your vision, stick to your purpose, and maintain your faith and gratitude. But you must act in a Certain Way, so that you can appropriate what is yours when it comes to you, so that you can meet the things you have in your picture and put them in their proper places as they arrive.

You can readily see the truth of this. When things reach you, they will be in the hands of other men, who will ask an equivalent for them. And you can only get what is yours by giving the other man what is his. Your pocketbook is not going to be transformed into a Fortunates's purse, which shall be always full of money without effort on your part. This is the crucial point in the science of getting rich—right here, where thought and personal action must be combined. There are very many people who, consciously or unconsciously, set the creative forces in action by the strength and persistence of their desires, but who remain poor because they do not provide for the reception of the thing they want when it comes.

By thought, the thing you want is brought to you; by action, you receive it. Whatever your action is to be, it is evident that you must act NOW. You cannot act in the past, and it is essential to the clearness of your mental vision that you dismiss the past from your mind. You cannot act in the future, for the future is not here yet. And you cannot tell how you will want to act in any future contingency until that contingency has arrived.

Because you are not in the right business or the right environment now, do not think that you must postpone action until you get into the right business or environment. And do not spend time in the present taking thought as to the best course in possible future emergencies when it arrives. If you act in the present with your mind on the future, your present action will be with a divided mind and will not be effective. Put your whole mind into present action.

Do not give your creative impulse to Original Substance and then sit down and wait for results; if you do, you will never get them. Act now. There is never any time but now, and there never will be any time but now. If you are ever to begin to make ready for the reception of what you want, you must begin now, and your action— whatever it is—must most likely be in your present business or employment and must be upon the persons and things in your present environment.

You cannot act where you are not; you cannot act where you have been, and you cannot act where you are going to be; you can act only where you are. Do not bother as to whether yesterday's work was well done or ill done; do today's work well. Do not try to do to-morrow's work now; there will be plenty of time to do that when you get to it. Do not try, by occult or mystical means, to act on people or things that are out of your reach. Do not wait for a change of environment before you act; get a change of environment by action. You can so act upon the environment in which you are now as to cause yourself to be transferred to a better environment.

Hold with faith and purpose the vision of yourself in the better environment, but act upon your present environment with all your heart, and with all your strength, and with all your mind. Do not spend any time in day dreaming or castle building; hold to the one vision of what you want and act NOW. Do not cast about seeking some new thing to do or some strange, unusual, or remarkable action to perform as a first step toward getting rich.

It is probable that your actions, at least for some time to come, will be those you have been performing for some time past, but you are to begin now to perform these actions in the Certain Way, which will surely make you rich. If you are engaged in some business and feel that it is not the right one for you, do not wait until you get into the right business before you begin to act.

Do not feel discouraged or sit down and lament because you are misplaced. No man was ever so misplaced but that he could find the right place, and no man ever became so involved in the wrong business but that he could get into the right business. Hold the vision of yourself in the right business, with the purpose to get into it and the faith that you will get into it and are getting into it, but ACT in your present business. Use your present business as the means of getting a better one, and use your present environment as the means of getting into a better one. Your vision of the right business, if held with faith and purpose, will cause the Supreme to move the right business toward you, and your action, if performed in the Certain Way, will cause you to move toward the business.

If you are an employee or wage earner and feel that you must change places in order to get what you want, do not "project" your thought into space and rely upon it to get you another job. It will probably fail to do so. Hold the vision of yourself in the job you want while you ACT with faith and purpose on the job you have, and you will certainly get the job you want.

Your vision and faith will set the creative force in motion to bring it toward you, and your action will cause the forces in your own environment to move you toward the place you want. In closing this chapter, we will add another statement to our syllabus:

- There is a thinking stuff from which all things are made and which, in its original state, permeates, penetrates, and fills the interspaces of the universe.
- A thought, in this substance, produces the thing that is imaged by the thought.
- Man can form things in his thought, and, by impressing his thoughts upon formless substance, can cause the thing he thinks about to be created.
- In order to do this, man must pass from the competitive to the creative mind; he must form a clear mental picture of the things he wants and hold this picture in his thoughts with the fixed PURPOSE to get what he wants and the unwavering FAITH that he does get what he wants, closing his mind to all that may tend to shake his purpose, dim his vision, or quench his faith.
- That he may receive what he wants when it comes, man must act NOW upon the people and things in his present environment.

~ 19 ~

EFFICIENT ACTION

You must use your thought as directed in previous chapters and begin to do what you can do where you are, and you must do ALL that you can do where you are. You can advance only by being larger than your present place, and no man is larger than his present place who leaves undone any of the work pertaining to that place. The world is advanced only by those who more than fill their present places.

If no man quite filled his present place, you can see that there must be a going backward in everything. Those who do not quite fill their present places are a dead weight upon society, government, commerce, and industry; they must be carried along by others at a great expense. The progress of the world is retarded only by those who do not fill the places they are holding; they belong to a former age and a lower stage or plane of life, and their tendency is toward degeneration. No society could advance if every man was smaller than his place; social evolution is guided by the law of physical and mental evolution. In the animal world, evolution is caused by excess of life.

When an organism has more life than can be expressed in the functions of its own plane, it develops the organs of a higher plane, and a new species is originated. There never would have been new species had there not been organisms which more than filled their places. The law is exactly the same for you; your getting rich depends upon your applying this principle to your own affairs.

Every day is either a successful day or a day of failure, and it is the successful days which get you what you want. If every day is a failure, you can never get rich, while if every day is a success, you cannot fail to get rich. If there is something that may be done today and you do not do it, you have failed in so far as that thing is concerned, and the consequences may be more disastrous than you imagine. You cannot foresee the results of even the most trivial act; you do not know the workings of all the forces that have been set moving in your behalf. Much may be depending on your doing some simple act; it may be the very thing which is to open the door of opportunity to very great possibilities. You can never know all the combinations which Supreme Intelligence is making for you in the world of things and of human affairs; your neglect or failure to do some small thing may cause a long delay in getting what you want.

Do, every day, ALL that can be done that day. There is, however, a limitation or qualification of the above that you must take into account. You are not to overwork nor to rush blindly into your business in the effort to do the greatest possible number of things in the shortest possible time. You are not to try to do tomorrow's work today nor to do a week's work in a day.

> It is really not the number of things you do but the EFFICIENCY of each separate action that counts.

Every act is, in itself, either a success or a failure. Every act is, in itself, either effective or inefficient. Every inefficient act is a failure, and if you spend your life in doing inefficient acts, your whole life will be a failure.

The more things you do, the worse for you if all your acts are inefficient ones. On the other hand, every efficient act is a success in itself, and if every act of your life is an efficient one, your whole life MUST be a success. The cause of failure is doing too many things in an inefficient manner and not doing enough things in an efficient manner.

You will see that it is a self-evident proposition that if you do not do any inefficient acts and if you do a sufficient number of efficient acts, you will become rich. If, now, it is possible for you to make each act an efficient one, you see again that the getting of riches is reduced to an exact science, like mathematics.

The matter turns, then, on the question whether you can make each separate act a success in itself. And this you can certainly do. You can make each act a success because All Power is working with you, and All Power cannot fail. Power is at your service, and to make each act efficient, you have only to put power into it.

Every action is either strong or weak, and when every one is strong, you are acting in the Certain Way which will make you rich. Every act can be made strong and efficient by holding your vision while you are doing it and putting the whole power of your FAITH and PURPOSE into it.

It is at this point that the people fail who separate mental power from personal action. They use the power of mind in one place and at one time, and they act in another place and at another time. So their acts are not successful in themselves; too many of them are inefficient. But if All Power goes into every act, no matter how commonplace, every act will be a success in itself, and as in the nature of things, every success opens the way to other successes, your progress toward what you want and the progress of what you want toward you will become increasingly rapid. Remember that successful action is cumulative in its results.

Since the desire for more life is inherent in all things, when a man begins to move toward larger life, more things attach themselves to him, and the influence of his desire is multiplied. Do every day all that you can do that day, and do each act in an efficient manner.

In saying that you must hold your vision while you are doing each act, however trivial or commonplace, I do not mean to say that it is necessary at all times to see the vision distinctly to its smallest details. It should be the work of your leisure hours to use your imagination on the details of your vision and to contemplate them until they are firmly fixed upon your memory.

If you wish speedy results, spend practically all your spare time in this practice. By continuous contemplation, you will get the picture of what you want, even to the smallest details, so firmly fixed upon your mind and so completely transferred to the mind of Formless Substance that in your working hours you need only to mentally refer to the picture to stimulate your faith and purpose and cause your best effort to be put forth. Contemplate your picture in your leisure hours until your consciousness is so full of it that you can grasp it instantly. You will become so enthused with its bright promises that the mere thought of it will call forth the strongest energies of your whole being.

Let us again repeat our syllabus and, by slightly changing the closing statements, bring it to the point we have now reached.

There is a thinking stuff from which all things are made and which, in its original state, permeates, penetrates, and fills the interspaces of the universe.

- A thought, in this substance, produces the thing that is imaged by the thought.
- Man can form things in his thought, and, by impressing his thought upon formless substance, can cause the thing he thinks about to be created.
- In order to do this, man must pass from the competitive to the creative mind; he must form a clear mental picture of the things he wants and do, with faith and purpose, all that can be done each day, doing each separate thing in an efficient manner.

~ 20 ~

GETTING INTO THE RIGHT BUSINESS

Success in any particular business depends, for one thing, upon your possessing in a well-developed state the faculties required in that business.

Without good musical faculty no one can succeed as a teacher of music; without well-developed mechanical faculties, no one can achieve great success in any of the mechanical trades; without tact and the commercial faculties, no one can succeed in mercantile pursuits. But to possess in a well-developed state the faculties required in your particular vocation does not insure getting rich. There are musicians who have remarkable talent and who yet remain poor; there are blacksmiths, carpenters, and so on who have excellent mechanical ability but who do not get rich; and there are merchants with good faculties for dealing with men who nevertheless fail.

The different faculties are tools; it is essential to have good tools, but it is also essential that the tools should be used in the Right Way. One man can take a sharp saw, a square, a good plane, and so on, and build a handsome article of furniture; another man can take the same tools and set to work to duplicate the article, but his production will be a botch. He does not know how to use good tools in a successful way.

The various faculties of your mind are the tools with which you must do the work which is to make you rich; it will be easier for you to succeed if you get into a business for which you are well equipped with mental tools.

Generally speaking, you will do best in that business which will use your strongest faculties—the one for which you are naturally "best fitted." But there are limitations to this statement, also. No man should regard his vocation as being irrevocably fixed by the tendencies with which he was born.

You can get rich in ANY business, for if you have not the right talent for it, you can develop that talent; it merely means that you will have to make your tools as you go along instead of confining yourself to the use of those with which you were born. It will be EASIER for you to succeed in a vocation for which you already have the talents in a well-developed state, but you CAN succeed in any vocation, for you can develop any rudimentary talent, and there is no talent of which you have not at least the rudiment.

You will get rich most easily in point of effort if you do that for which you are best fitted, but you will get rich most satisfactorily if you do that which you WANT to do.

Doing what you want to do is life, and there is no real satisfaction in living if we are compelled to be forever doing something which we do not like to do and can never do what we want to do. And it is certain that you can do what you want to do; the desire to do it is proof that you have within you the power which can do it.

Desire is a manifestation of power. The desire to play music is the power which can play music, seeking expression and development; the desire to invent mechanical devices is the mechanical talent seeking expression and development.

Where there is no power, either developed or undeveloped, to do a thing, there is never any desire to do that thing, and where there is strong desire to do a thing, it is certain proof that the"power to do it is strong and only requires to be developed and applied in the Right Way.

All things else being equal, it is best to select the business for which you have the best developed talent, but if you have a strong desire to engage in any particular line of work, you should select that work as the ultimate end at which you aim. You can do what you want to do, and it is your right and privilege to follow the business or avocation which will be most congenial and pleasant.

You are not obliged to do what you do not like to do and should not do it except as a means to bring you to the doing of the thing you want to do. If there are past mistakes whose consequences have placed you in an undesirable business or environment, you may be obliged for some time to do what you do not like to do, but you can make the doing of it pleasant by knowing that it is making it possible for you to come to the doing of what you want to do.

If you feel that you are not in the right vocation, do not act too hastily in trying to get into another one. The best way, generally, to change business or environment is by growth.

Do not be afraid to make a sudden and radical change if the opportunity is presented and you feel after careful consideration that it is the right opportunity; but never take sudden or radical action when you are in doubt as to the wisdom of doing so. There is never any hurry on the creative plane, and there is no lack of opportunity.

When you get out of the competitive mind you will understand that you never need to act hastily. No one else is going to beat you to the thing you want to do; there is enough for all. If one place is taken, another and a better one will be opened for you a little farther on; there is plenty of time. When you are in doubt, wait. Fall back on the contemplation of your vision and increase your faith and purpose; and by all means, in times of doubt and indecision, cultivate gratitude.

A day or two spent in contemplating the vision of what you want and in earnest thanksgiving that you are getting it will bring your mind into such close relationship with the Supreme that you will make no mistake when you do act.

There is a mind which knows all there is to know, and you can come into close unity with this mind by faith and the purpose to advance in life if you have deep gratitude.

Mistakes come from acting hastily, or from acting in fear or doubt, or in forgetfulness of the Right Motive, which is more life to all and less to none.

As you go on in the Certain Way, opportunities will come to you in increasing number; and you will need to be very steady in your faith and purpose and to keep in close touch with the All Mind by reverent gratitude.

Do all that you can do in a perfect manner every day, but do it without haste, worry, or fear. Go as fast as you can, but never hurry.

Remember that in the moment you begin to hurry, you cease to be a creator and become a competitor; you drop back upon the old plane again.

Whenever you find yourself hurrying, call a halt, fix your attention on the mental image of the thing you want, and begin to give thanks that you are getting it. The exercise of GRATITUDE will never fail to strengthen your faith and renew your purpose.

~ 21 ~

THE IMPRESSION OF INCREASE

Whether you change your vocation or not, your actions for the present must be those pertaining to the business in which you are now engaged. You can get into the business you want by making constructive use of the business you are already established in; by doing your daily work in a Certain Way.

And in so far as your business consists in dealing with other men, whether personally or by letter, the key thought of all your efforts must be to convey to their minds the impression of increase.

Increase is what all men and all women are seeking; it is the urge of the Formless Intelligence within them, seeking fuller expression.

The desire for increase is inherent in all nature; it is the fundamental impulse of the universe. All human activities are based on the desire for increase; people are seeking more food, more clothes, better shelter, more luxury, more beauty, more knowledge, more pleasure—increase in something, more life.

Every living thing is under this necessity for continuous advancement; where increase of life ceases, dissolution and death set in at once.

Man instinctively knows this, and hence he is forever seeking more. This law of perpetual increase is set forth by Jesus in the parable of the talents: only those who gain more retain any; from him who hath not shall be taken away even that which he hath.

The normal desire for increased wealth is not an evil or a rep-rehensible thing; it is simply the desire for more abundant life; it is aspiration. And because it is the deepest instinct of their natures, all men and women are attracted to him who can give them more of the means of life.

In following the Certain Way as described in the foregoing pages, you are getting continuous increase for yourself, and you are giving it to all with whom you deal. You are a creative center, from which increase is given off to all. Be sure of this and convey assurance of the fact to every man, woman, and child with whom you come in contact. No matter how small the transaction, even if it be only the selling of a stick of candy to a little child, put into it the thought of increase, and make sure that the customer is impressed with the thought.

Convey the impression of advancement with everything you do, so that all people shall receive the impression that you are an Advancing Man, and that you advance all who deal with you. Even to the people whom you meet in a social way without any thought of business and to whom you do not try to sell anything, give the thought of increase.

You can convey this impression by holding the unshakable faith that you, yourself, are in the Way of Increase and by letting this faith inspire, fill, and permeate every action.

Do everything that you do in the firm conviction that you are an advancing personality and that you are giving advancement to everybody.

Feel that you are getting rich and that, in so doing, you are making others rich and conferring benefits on all.

Do not boast or brag of your success or talk about it unneces-sarily; true faith is never boastful. Wherever you find a boastful person, you find one who is secretly doubtful and afraid. Simply feel the faith and let it work out in every transaction; let every act, tone, and look express the quiet assurance that you are getting rich; that you are already rich. Words will not be necessary to communicate this feeling to others; they will feel the sense of increase when in your presence and will be attracted to you again.

You must so impress others that they will feel that in associating with you, they will get increase for themselves. See that you give them a use value greater than the cash value you are taking from them.

Take an honest pride in doing this and let everybody know it, and you will have no lack of customers. People will go where they are given increase, and the Supreme, which desires increase in all and which knows all, will move toward you, men and women who have never heard of you. Your business will increase rapidly, and you will be surprised at the unexpected benefits which will come to you. You will be able from day to day to make larger combinations, secure greater advantages, and to go on into a more congenial vocation if you desire to do so.

But in doing all this, you must never lose sight of your vision of what you want or your faith and purpose to get what you want. Let me here give you another word of caution in regard to motives. Beware of the insidious temptation to seek for power over other men. Nothing is so pleasant to the unformed or partially developed mind as the exercise of power or dominion over others. The desire to rule for selfish gratification has been the curse of the world. For countless ages, kings and lords have drenched the earth with blood in their battles to extend their dominions—not to seek more life for all, but to get more power for themselves.

Today, the main motive in the business and industrial world is the same: men marshal their armies of dollars and lay waste the lives and hearts of millions in the same mad scramble for power over others. Commercial kings, like political kings, are inspired by the lust for power. Jesus saw in this desire for mastery the moving impulse of that evil world He sought to overthrow. Read the twenty-third chapter of Matthew and see how He pictures the lust of the Pharisees to be called "Master," to sit in the high places, to domineer over others, and to lay burdens on the backs of the less fortunate; and note how He compares this lust for dominion with the brotherly seeking for the Common Good to which He calls His disciples.

Look out for the temptation to seek for authority, to become a "master," to be considered as one who is above the common herd, to impress others by lavish display, and so on.

The mind that seeks for mastery over others is the competitive mind, and the competitive mind is not the creative one. In order to master your environment and your destiny, it is not at all necessary that you should rule over your fellow men, and indeed, when you fall into the world's struggle for the high places, you begin to be conquered by fate and environment, and your getting rich becomes a matter of chance and speculation.

Beware of the competitive mind! No better statement of the principle of creative action can be formulated than the favorite declaration of the late "Golden Rule" Jones of Toledo: "What I want for myself, I want for everybody."

~ 22 ~

THE ADVANCING MAN

What I have said in the last chapter applies as well to the professional man and the wage-earner as to the man who is engaged in mercantile business.

No matter whether you are a physician, a teacher, or a clergyman, if you can give increase of life to others and make them sensible of the fact, they will be attracted to you, and you will get rich. The physician who holds the vision of himself as a great and successful healer and who works toward the complete realization of that vision with faith and purpose, as described in former chapters, will come into such close touch with the Source of Life that he will be phenomenally successful; patients will come to him in throngs.

No one has a greater opportunity to carry into effect the teachings of this book than the practitioner of medicine; it does not matter to which of the various schools he may belong, for the principle of healing is common to all of them and may be reached by all alike. The Advancing Man in medicine, who holds to a clear mental image of himself as successful and who obeys the laws of faith, purpose, and gratitude, will cure every curable case he undertakes, no matter what remedies he may use.

In the field of religion, the world cries out for the clergyman who can teach his hearers the true science of abundant life. He who masters the details of the science of getting rich, together with the allied sciences of being well, of being great, and of winning love, and who teaches these details from the pulpit, will never lack for a congregation. This is the gospel that the world needs; it will give increase of life, and men will hear it gladly and will give liberal support to the man who brings it to them.

What is now needed is a demonstration of the science of life from the pulpit. We want preachers who can not only tell us how but who, in their own words, will show us how. We need the preacher, who will himself be rich, healthy, great, and beloved, to teach us how to attain to these things, and when he comes, he will find a numerous and loyal following.

The same is true of the teacher, who can inspire the children with the faith and purpose of the advancing life. He will never be "out of a job." And any teacher who has this faith and purpose can give it to his pupils; he cannot help giving it to them if it is part of his own life and practice.

What is true of the teacher, preacher, and physician is true of the lawyer, dentist, real estate man, insurance agent—of everybody. The combined mental and personal action I have described is infallible; it cannot fail. Every man and woman who follows these instructions steadily, perseveringly, and to the letter will get rich. The law of the Increase of Life is as mathematically certain in its operation as the law of gravitation; getting rich is an exact science.

The wage-earner will find this as true of his case as of any of the others mentioned. Do not feel that you have no chance to get rich because you are working where there is no visible opportunity for advancement, where wages are small, and the cost of living high. Form your clear mental vision of what you want and begin to act with faith and purpose. Do all the work you can do every day, and do each piece of work in a perfectly successful manner; put the power of success and the purpose to get rich into everything you do. But do not do this merely with the idea of currying favor with your employer in the hope that he, or those above you, will see your good work and advance you; it is not likely that they will do so.

The man who is merely a "good" workman, filling his place to the very best of his ability and satisfied with that, is valuable to his employer, and it is not to the employer's interest to promote him; he is worth more where he is. To secure advancement, something more is necessary than to be too large for your place. The man who is certain to advance is the one who is too big for his place, and who has a clear concept of what he wants to be, who knows that he can become what he wants to be, and who is determined to BE what he wants to be.

Do not try to more than fill your present place with a view to pleasing your employer; do it with the idea of advancing yourself. Hold the faith and purpose of increase during work hours, after work hours, and before work hours. Hold it in such a way that every person who comes in contact with you, whether foreman, fellow workman, or social acquaintance, will feel the power of purpose radiating from you, so that every one will get the sense of advancement and increase from you. Men will be attracted to you, and if there is no possibility for advancement in your present job, you will very soon see an opportunity to take another job.

There is a Power which never fails to present opportunity to the Advancing Man who is moving in obedience to law. God cannot help helping you, if you act in a Certain Way; He must do so in order to help Himself. There is nothing in your circumstances or in the industrial situation that can keep you down. If you cannot get rich working for the steel trust, you can get rich on a ten-acre farm, and if you begin to move in the Certain Way, you will certainly escape from the "clutches" of the steel trust and get on to the farm or wherever else you wish to be.

If a few thousands of its employees would enter upon the Certain Way, the steel trust would soon be in a bad plight; it would have to give its workingmen more opportunity or go out of business. Nobody has to work for a trust; the trusts can keep men in so-called hopeless conditions only so long as there are men who are too ignorant to know of the science of getting rich or too intellectually slothful to practice it.

Begin this way of thinking and acting, and your faith and purpose will make you quick to see any opportunity to better your condition.

Such opportunities will speedily come, for the Supreme, working in All, and working for you, will bring them before you.

Do not wait for an opportunity to be all that you want to be; when an opportunity to be more than you are now is presented and you feel impelled toward it, take it. It will be the first step toward a greater opportunity.

There is no such thing possible in this universe as a lack of opportunities for the man who is living the advancing life.

It is inherent in the constitution of the cosmos that all things shall be for him and work together for his good, and he must certainly get rich if he acts and thinks in the Certain Way. So let wage-earning men and women study this book with great care and enter with confidence upon the course of action it prescribes; it will not fail.

~ 23 ~

SOME CAUTIONS & CONCLUDING
OBSERVATIONS

Many people will scoff at the idea that there is an exact science of getting rich; holding the impression that the supply of wealth is limited, they will insist that social and governmental institutions must be changed before even any considerable number of people can acquire a competence.

But this is not true. It is true that existing governments keep the masses in poverty, but this is because the masses do not think and act in the Certain Way.

If the masses begin to move forward as suggested in this book, neither governments nor industrial systems can check them; all systems must be modified to accommodate the forward movement.

If the people have the Advancing Mind, have the Faith that they can become rich, and move forward with the fixed purpose to become rich, nothing can possibly keep them in poverty. Individuals may enter upon the Certain Way at any time and under any government and make themselves rich, and when any considerable number of individuals do so under any government, they will cause the system to be so modified as to open the way for others.

The more men who get rich on the competitive plane, the worse for others; the more who get rich on the creative plane, the better for others.

The economic salvation of the masses can only be accomplished by getting a large number of people to practice the scientific method set down in this book and become rich. These will show others the way and inspire them with a desire for real life, with the faith that it can be attained, and with the purpose to attain it.

For the present, however, it is enough to know that neither the government under which you live nor the capitalistic or competitive system of industry can keep you from getting rich. When you enter upon the creative plane of thought, you will rise above all these things and become a citizen of another kingdom. But remember that your thought must be held upon the creative plane; you are never for an instant to be betrayed into regarding the supply as limited or into acting on the moral level of competition.

Whenever you do fall into old ways of thought, correct yourself instantly, for when you are in the competitive mind, you have lost the co-operation of the Mind of the Whole. Do not spend any time in planning as to how you will meet possible emergencies in the future, except as the necessary policies may affect your actions to-day. You are concerned with doing to-day's work in a perfectly successful manner and not with emergencies which may arise to-morrow; you can attend to them as they come.

Do not concern yourself with questions as to how you shall surmount obstacles which may loom upon your business horizon unless you can see plainly that your course must be altered to-day in order to avoid them.

No matter how tremendous an obstruction may appear at a distance, you will find that if you go on in the Certain way, it will disappear as you approach it or that a way over, through, or around it will appear.

No possible combination of circumstances can defeat a man or woman who is proceeding to get rich along strictly scientific lines. No man or woman who obeys the law can fail to get rich, any more than one can multiply two by two and fail to get four.

Give no anxious thought to possible disasters, obstacles, panics, or unfavorable combinations of circumstances; it is time enough to meet such things when they present themselves before you in the immediate present, and you will find that every difficulty carries with it the wherewithal for its overcoming.

Guard your speech. Never speak of yourself, your affairs, or of anything else in a discouraged or discouraging way. Never admit the possibility of failure or speak in a way that infers failure as a possibility.

Never speak of the times as being hard or of business conditions as being doubtful. Times may be hard and business doubtful for those who are on the competitive plane, but they can never be so for you; you can create what you want, and you are above fear.

When others are having hard times and poor business, you will find your greatest opportunities. Train yourself to think of and to look upon the world as a something which is Becoming, which is growing, and to regard seeming evil as being only that which is un-developed. Always speak in terms of advancement; to do otherwise is to deny your faith, and to deny your faith is to lose it.

Never allow yourself to feel disappointed. You may expect to have a certain thing at a certain time and not get it at that time, and this will appear to you like failure. But if you hold to your faith you will find that the failure is only apparent. Go on in the certain way, and if you do not receive that thing, you will receive something so much better that you will see that the seeming failure was really a great success.

A student of this science had set his mind on making a certain business combination which seemed to him at the time to be very desirable, and he worked for some weeks to bring it about. When the crucial time came, the thing failed in a perfectly inexplicable way; it was as if some unseen influence had been working secretly against him. He was not disappointed; on the contrary, he thanked God that his desire had been overruled and went steadily on with a grateful mind. In a few weeks, an opportunity so much better came his way that he would not have made the first deal on any account, and he saw that a Mind which knew more than he knew had prevented him from losing the greater good by entangling himself with the lesser.

That is the way every seeming failure will work out for you if you keep your faith, hold to your purpose, have gratitude, and do every day all that can be done that day, doing each separate act in a successful manner.

When you make a failure, it is because you have not asked for enough. keep on, and a larger thing than you were seeking will certainly come to you. Remember this.

You will not fail because you lack the necessary talent to do what you wish to do. If you go on as I have directed, you will develop all the talent that is necessary to the doing of your work. It is not within the scope of this book to deal with the science of cultivating talent, but it is as certain and simple as the process of getting rich. However, do not hesitate or waver for fear that when you come to any certain place you will fail for lack of ability; keep right on, and when you come to that place, the ability will be furnished to you. The same source of Ability which enabled the untaught Lincoln to do the greatest work in government ever accomplished by a single man is open to you; you may draw upon all the mind there is for wisdom to use in meeting the responsibilities which are laid upon you. Go on in full faith.

Study this book. Make it your constant companion until you have mastered all the ideas contained in it. While you are getting firmly established in this faith, you will do well to give up most recreations and pleasures and to stay away from places where ideas conflicting with these are advanced in lectures or sermons. Do not read pessimistic or conflicting literature or get into arguments upon the matter. Do very little reading outside of the writers mentioned in the Preface. Spend most of your leisure time in contemplating your vision, and in cultivating gratitude, and in reading this book. It contains all you need to know of the science of getting rich, and you will find all the essentials summed up in the following chapter.

~ 24 ~

SUMMARY OF THE SCIENCE OF
GETTING RICH

There is a thinking stuff from which all things are made and which, in its original state, permeates, penetrates, and fills the interspaces of the universe. A thought in this substance produces the thing that is imaged by the thought.

Man can form things in his thought, and by impressing his thought upon formless substance can cause the thing he thinks about to be created.

In order to do this, man must pass from the competitive to the creative mind; otherwise, he cannot be in harmony with the Formless Intelligence, which is always creative and never competitive in spirit.

Man may come into full harmony with the Formless Substance by entertaining a lively and sincere gratitude for the blessings it bestows upon him. Gratitude unifies the mind of man with the intelligence of Substance, so that man's thoughts are received by the Formless. Man can remain upon the creative plane only by uniting himself with the Formless Intelligence through a deep and continuous feeling of gratitude.

Man must form a clear and definite mental image of the things he wishes to have, to do, or to become, and he must hold this mental image in his thoughts while being deeply grateful to the Supreme that all his desires are granted to him. The man who wishes to get rich must spend his leisure hours in contemplating his Vision, and in earnest thanksgiving that the reality is being given to him. Too much stress cannot be laid on the importance of frequent contemplation of the mental image, coupled with unwavering faith and devout gratitude. This is the process by which the impression is given to the Formless, and the creative forces set in motion.

The creative energy works through the established channels of natural growth and of the industrial and social order. All that is included in his mental image will surely be brought to the man who follows the instructions given above and whose faith does not waver. What he wants will come to him through the ways of established trade and commerce.

In order to receive his own when it shall come to him, man must be active, and this activity can only consist in more than filling his present place. He must keep in mind the Purpose to get rich through the realization of his mental image. And he must do, every day, all that can be done that day, taking care to do each act in a successful manner. He must give to every man a use value in excess of the cash value he receives, so that each transaction makes for more life, and he must so hold the Advancing Thought that the impression of Increase will be communicated to all with whom he comes in contact.

The men and women who practice the foregoing instructions will certainly get rich, and the riches they receive will be in exact proportion to the definiteness of their vision, the fixity of their purpose, the steadiness of their faith, and the depth of their gratitude.

Conclusion

By Fenwicke Holmes & Shirley Smolko

The universe is real; matter is real; things are thoughts, or, to be more accurate, are Mind taking form through thought. We can control our world of interest because of the intelligence in it that is obedient to thought, provided we are conscious of the facts we have learned in the preceding chapters that, in our potential nature, we are one with the Infinite Creative Mind.

Finally, we should observe that intelligence acts on an impersonal basis, creating the pattern that our thought affords to it. It is entirely neutral, and we may mold substance by our thought either into magnificent physical manhood and womanhood or into deformed, emaciated, and cancerous flesh. Our word or thought is literally "made flesh and dwells among us." We get out of our universe what we put into it, for it reflects our moods and thoughts. Good and evil are alike real as effects, but they are simply the outer expression of inner concepts. And you live in an eternal, undying universe, for though form and thought may change, the primary substance can never pass away. The primary substance is Mind, and as you share in It, you too are eternally at one with It.

—Fenwick Holmes

The greatest power in the world is the power of our thought. Nothing exists that did not first exist in thought from the first sun that blazed only in the Mind of the Creator to the first airplane created in the minds of the Wright brothers. Mind in action is called the law of cause and effect. Law is the principle on which the mind works. Thought is the first cause, and form is the effect. Thoughts act upon substance to produce things. Substance is pure energy with the potential to become whatever we impress upon it. The things created by our thoughts maintain form and reality for as long as they are sustained by the original thought.

Therefore, the secret to *The Science of Getting Rich* is knowing how to form and sustain energy with thoughts that create wealth, along with acting in a certain way by connecting thought with personal action. For instance, you must open a channel for riches to flow to you—such as a business or investment—if you expect to get rich!

Shirley Smolko, MBA, MSA

About Shirley Smolko

S hirley Smolko, also known as *The Venetian Medium*, is a natural Psychic Medium, which means she was born with the ability to perceive psychic information and communicate with the souls of people who have passed away. In addition to being a Psychic Medium, she is a publisher, author, and lecturer.

She holds a Bachelor of Science in Nursing, a Masters in Business Administration, and another Masters degree in the Science of Accounting. She is also certified in grief counseling.

Shirley lives in the USA with her husband, Joe, and two cats, Zoey and Cecilia. You can find out more about Shirley, her books, and what she is up to by going to venetianmedium.com or cavallaropub.com.

Books By Shirley Smolko (As Of This Printing):

- *My Adventures as a Psychic Nurse & Medium: Spirits Everywhere!* (Previously published as *Adventures of a Psychic Nurse: Spirits Everywhere!*)
- *My Adventures as a Psychic Nurse & Medium: Haunted Hospital!* (Previously published as: *More Adventures of a Psychic Nurse: Haunted Hospitals!*)
- *Just a Thought Away: Communicating With Loved Ones In Spirit*
- *Money Wants Me!*
- *Money at Your Command!*
- *Secret to the Science of Getting Rich*
- *At Your Command!*
- *Revelations of the Afterlife: A New Arrival*

Be Sure to Look for More Books to Come!

ABOUT FENWICKE HOLMES

Fenwicke Lindsay Holmes was an American author, lecturer, writer, former Congregational minister, and Religious Science leader. He was also the brother of Religious Science founder Ernest Holmes. Fenwicke was born on a farm near Lincoln, Maine. Fenwicke attended Colby College in Waterville, Maine, while working several jobs to pay for his tuition. He graduated with a Bachelor of Arts degree in 1906.

He later founded a Congregational Church in Venice, California, where he ministered for six years. In 1912, he convinced his brother Ernest to join him. The brothers began extensively studying New Thought, in particular the ideas of Thomas Troward and, a few years later, New Thought leader Christian D. Larson. In 1917, Fenwicke resigned as minister from the Congregational Church because of his newfound beliefs, which were heavily influenced by the writings of New Thought movement leader William Walker Atkinson.

In 1927, Fenwicke helped his brother, Ernest, found the Institute of Religious Science and School of Philosophy as a means of spreading their teachings. After that, he ministered at the Divine Science Church of the Healing Christ in New York City until 1934. Then Fenwick and his wife moved to Santa Monica, California, where he became president of the International College of Mental Science and continued lecturing.

In the 1950s, Holmes collaborated with Dr. Masaharu Taniguchi in founding the Japanese New Thought organization Seicho-No-Ie and co-authored its guiding book, *The Science of Faith*.

Books by Fenwick Holmes:

Healing At A Distance *(1917)*

The Law of Mind in Action: Daily Lessons and Treatments in Mental and Spiritual Science *(1919)*

Visualization, Concentration, and How to Choose a Career (1922)

How to Develop Faith That Heals *(1919)*

Practical Healing *(1921)*

The Unfailing Formula *(1919)*

Being and Becoming: A Book of Lessons in the Science of Mind, Showing How to Find the Personal Spirit *(1919)*

Songs of the Silence and Other Poems *(1921)*

How to Solve Your Personal Problem: The God-Law and the Key to Power *(1934)*

Religion and Mental Science: Lyrics of Life and Love *(1925)*

Text Book of Practical Healing: The "Just How Course" in Healing the Mental Science Way *(1943)*

Healing Treatments in Verse *(1943)*

A Tiny Textbook of Meditation and the Lord's Prayer *(1943)*

Calm Yourself: A Key to Serenity *(1949)*

The Tiny Textbook of Mental Healing *(1951)*

The Science of Faith: How to Make Yourself Believe, Masaharu Taniguchi *(1952)*

Philip's cousin Jesus: the untold story *(1970)*

Psycho-Dietetics: How to Eat, Drink, and Think for Health, including the Holmes Food Chemistry and Vitamins

Being and Becoming *(1883)*

ABOUT WALLACE D. WATTLES

Wattles' daughter, Florence A. Wattles, described her father's life in a "Letter" that was published shortly after his death in the New Thought magazine *Nautilus,* edited by Elizabeth Towne. *The Nautilus* had previously carried articles by Wattles in almost every issue, and Towne was also his book publisher. Florence Wattles wrote that her father was born in the U.S. in 1860, received little formal education, and found himself excluded from the world of commerce and wealth.

According to the 1880 US Federal Census, Wallace lived with his parents on a farm in Nunda Township, McHenry County, Illinois, and worked as a farm laborer. His father is listed as a gardener and his mother as "keeping house". Wallace is listed as being born in Illinois, while his parents are listed as being born in New York. No other siblings are recorded as living with the family. According to the 1910 census, Wattles was married to Abbie Wattles (née Bryant), 47. They had three children: Florence Wattles, 22, Russell H. Wattles, 27, and Agnes Wattles, 16. It also shows that at the time, Wallace's mother, Mary A. Wattles, was living with the family at the age of 79.

Florence wrote that "he made lots of money and had good health, except for his extreme frailty" in the last three years before his death. Wattles died on February 7, 1911, in Ruskin, Tennessee, and his body was transported home for burial in Elwood, Indiana. As a sign of respect, businesses closed throughout the town for two hours on the afternoon of his funeral.

His death at age 51 was regarded as "untimely" by his daughter; in the previous year he had not only published two books (*The Science of Being Well* and *The Science of Getting Rich*), but he had also run for public office.

- Wattles, W. D. (1904). *Scientific marriage*. Marion, Ind.: W.D. Wattles
- Wattles, W. D. (1905). *Jesus, the man, and his work* Cincinnati? (A long speech made into a pamphlet and the basis of "A New Christ").
- Wattles, W. D. (1907). *The new science of living and healing* Holyoke, Mass.: Elizabeth Towne republished as **Health Through New Thought and Fasting* (Elizabeth Towne, 1924)
- Wattles, W. D. (1909). *Making the man who can* Holyoke, Mass.: Elizabeth Towne, 15166857. republished later as Elizabeth Towne, May 5, 1914.
- Wattles, W. D. (1910). *What Is Truth?* (1909)
- Wattles, W. D. (1910). "Perpetual Youth" (1909, in *The Cavalier).*
- Wattles, W. D. (1910). *A new Christ* United States: publisher not identified
- Wattles, W. D. (1910). *Hell-fire Harrison... Illustrated and decorated in colors by Frank T. Merrill.* Boston: L. C. Page & Co.
- Wattles, W. D. (c. 1910) *Letters to a Woman's Husband* (pamphlet)
- Wattles, W. D. (c. 1910) *The Constructive Use of Foods* (pamphlet)
- Wattles, W. D. (n. d.). *How to get what you want* Holyoke, Mass.: Elizabeth Towne Co.

"The Science of" trilogy:

- Wattles, W. D. (1910). *The Science of Getting Rich* Holyoke, Mass.: E. Towne Republished posthumously in 1915 as *Financial Success Through Creative Thought.* San Gabriel, Calif.; Los Angeles: Willing; Distributed by Scrivener.

• Wattles, W. D. (1910). *The science of being well* Holyoke, Mass.: Towne.
• Wattles, W. D. (1911). *The science of being great* Holyoke, Mass.: E. Towne

www.ingramcontent.com/pod-product-compliance
Lightning Source LLC
Chambersburg PA
CBHW071203120626
46546CB00006B/2387